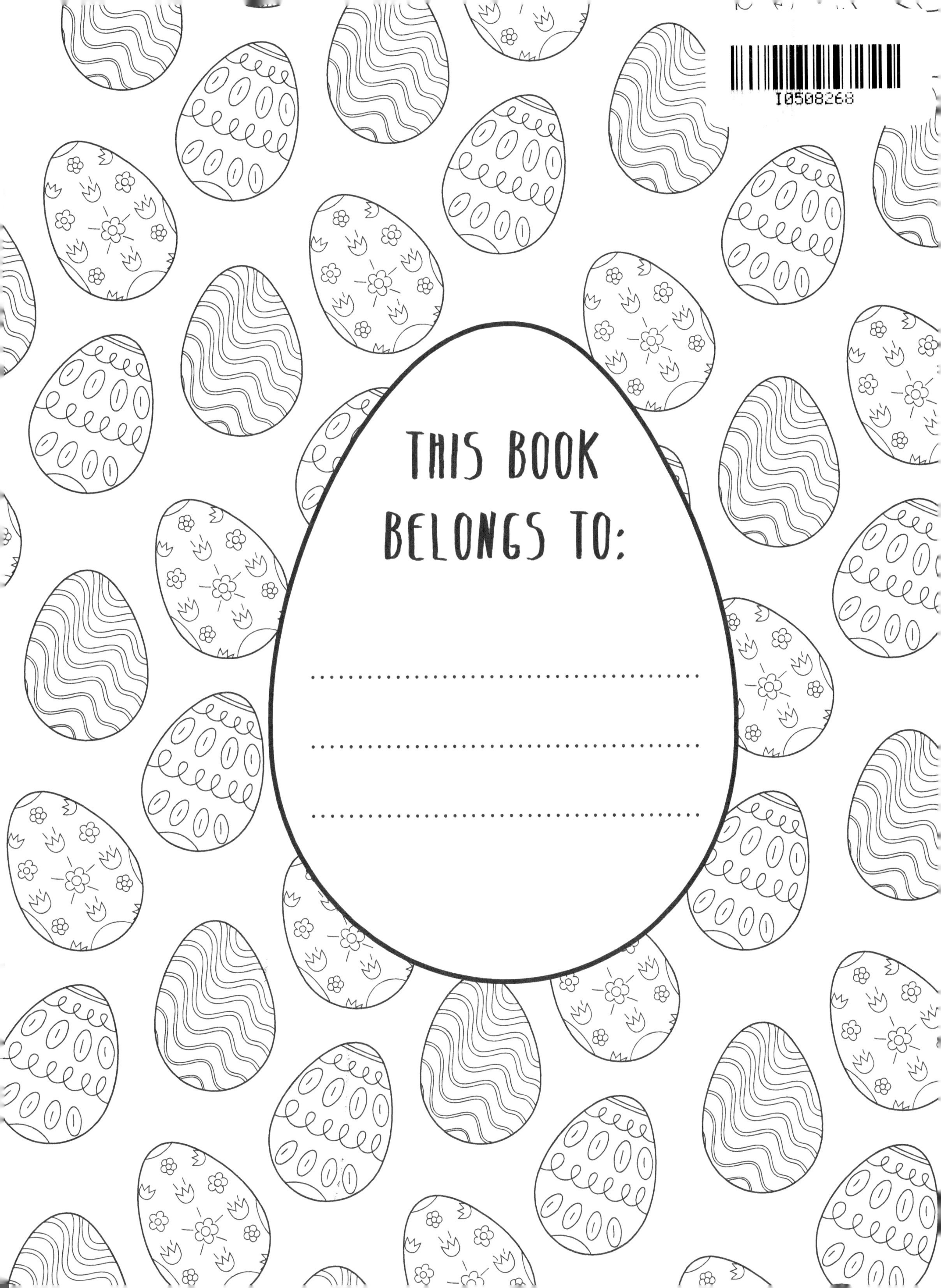
THIS BOOK
BELONGS TO:
....
....
....

COLOR TEST PAGE

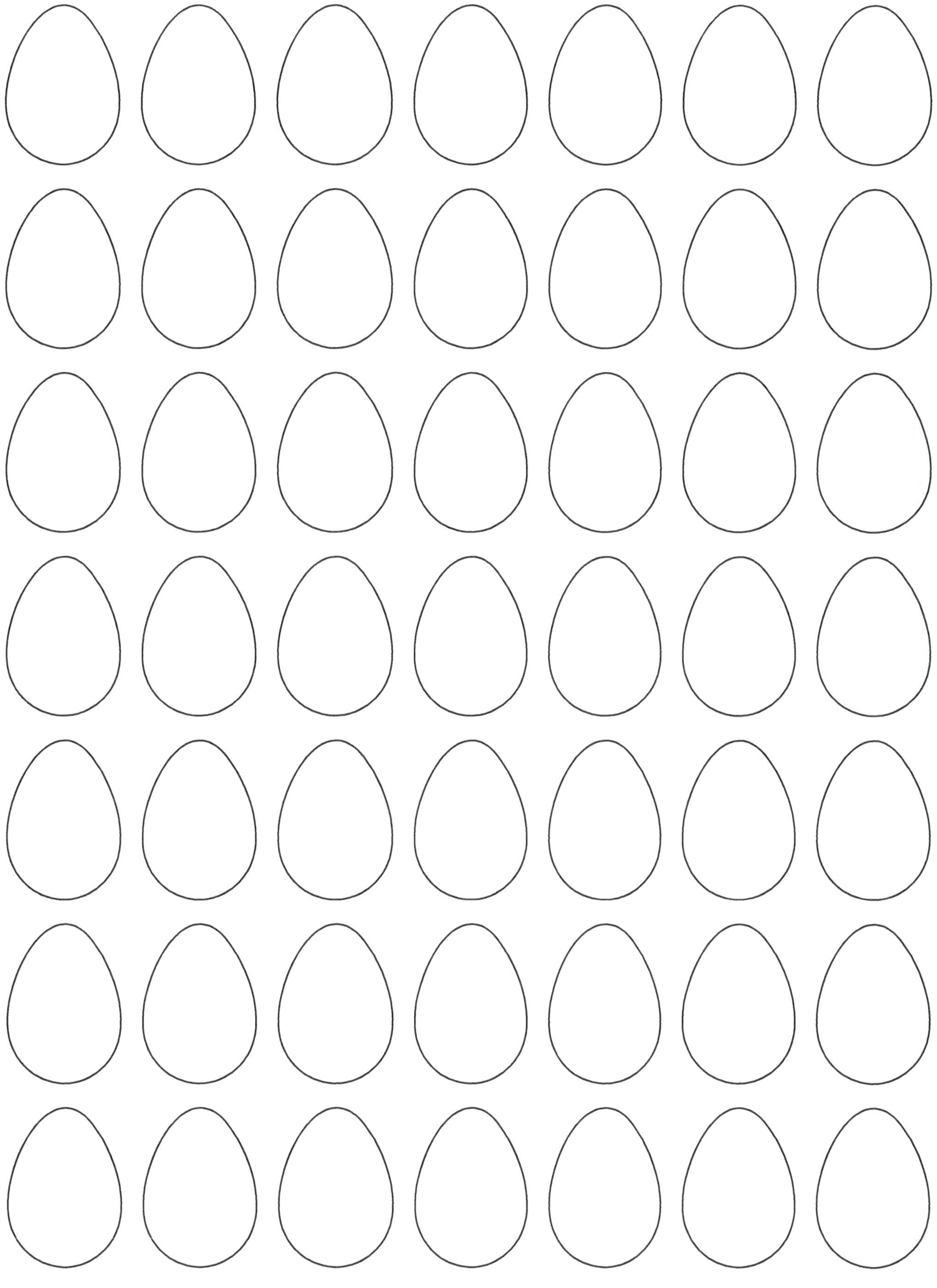

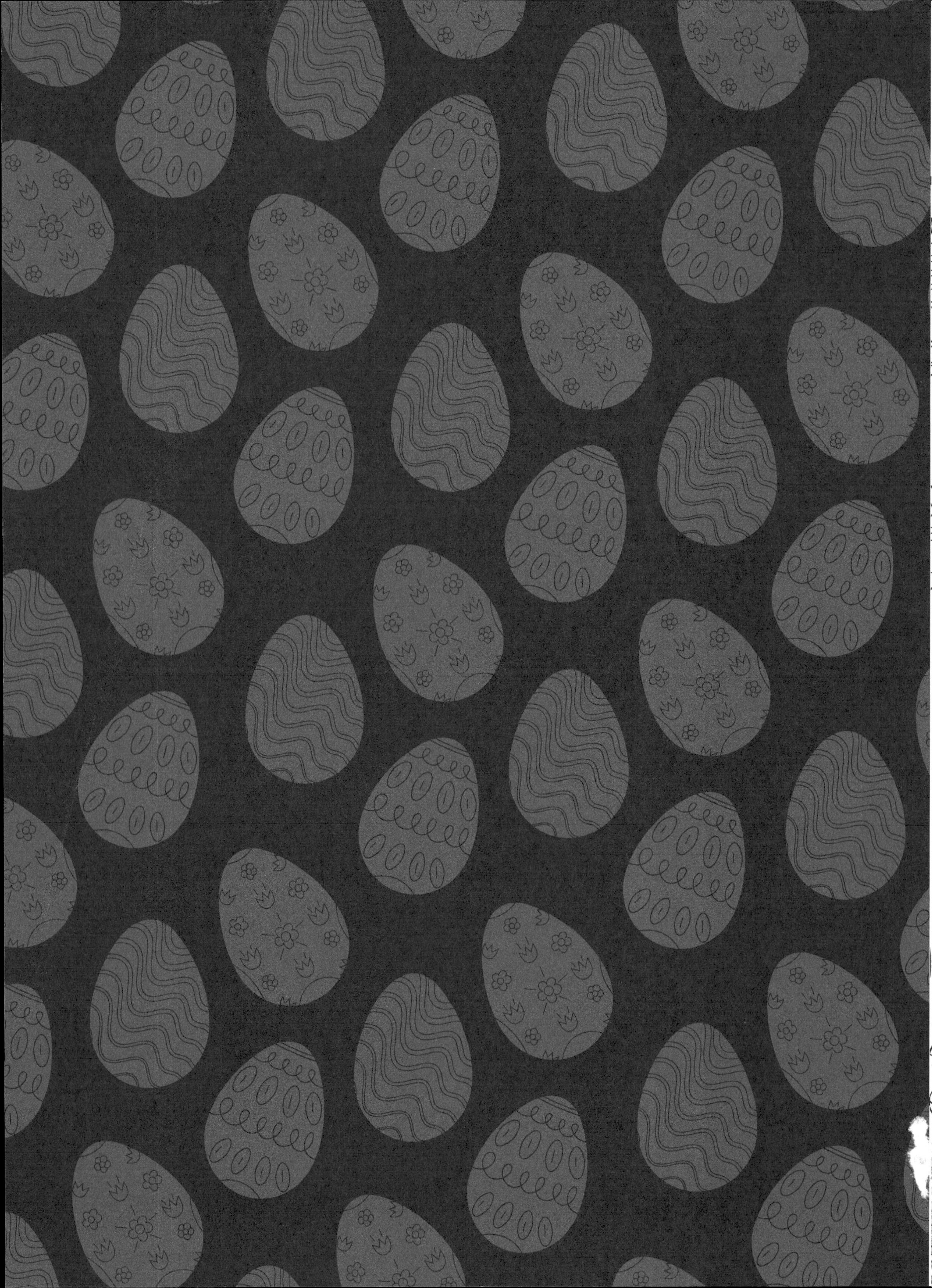

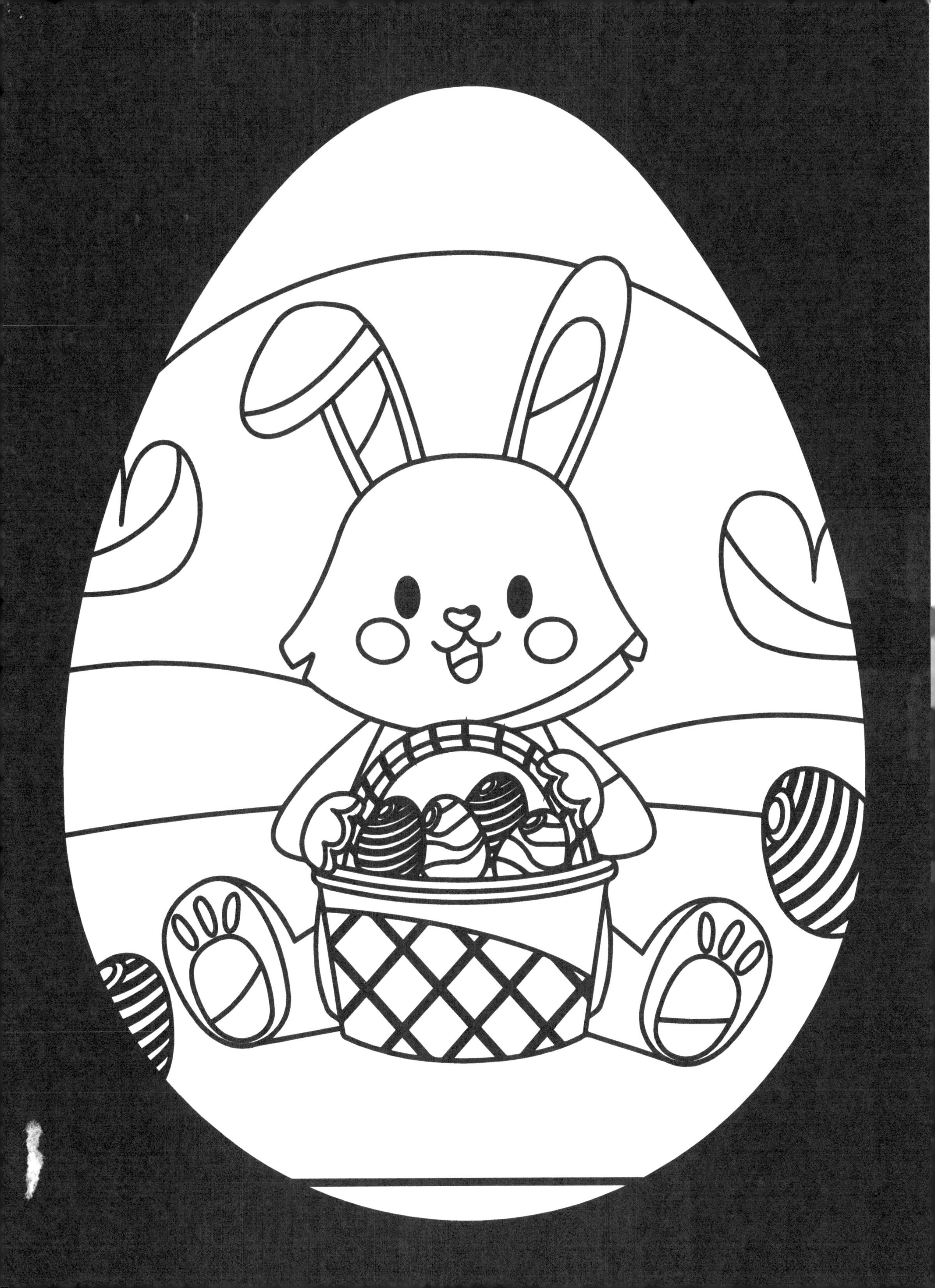

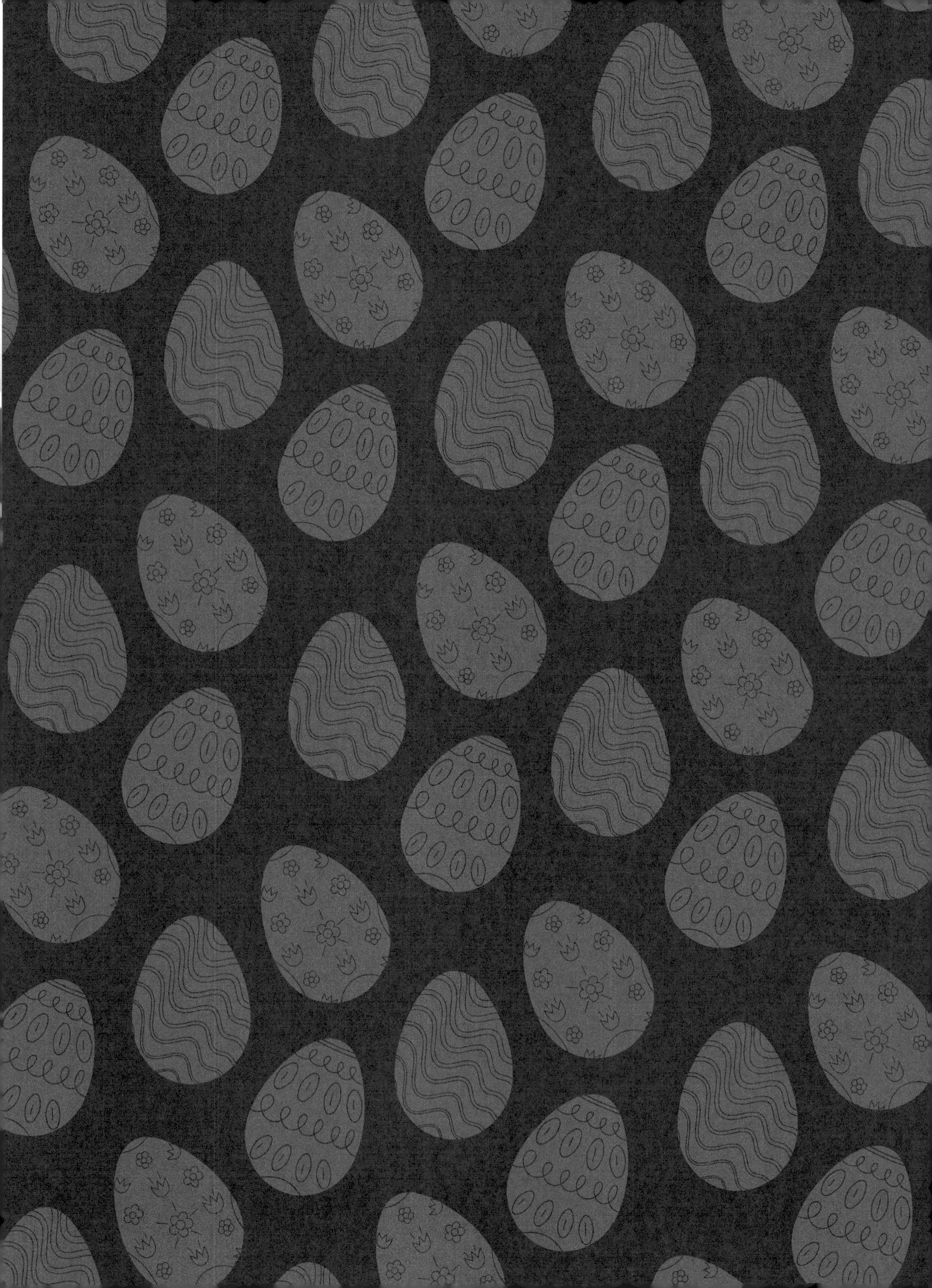

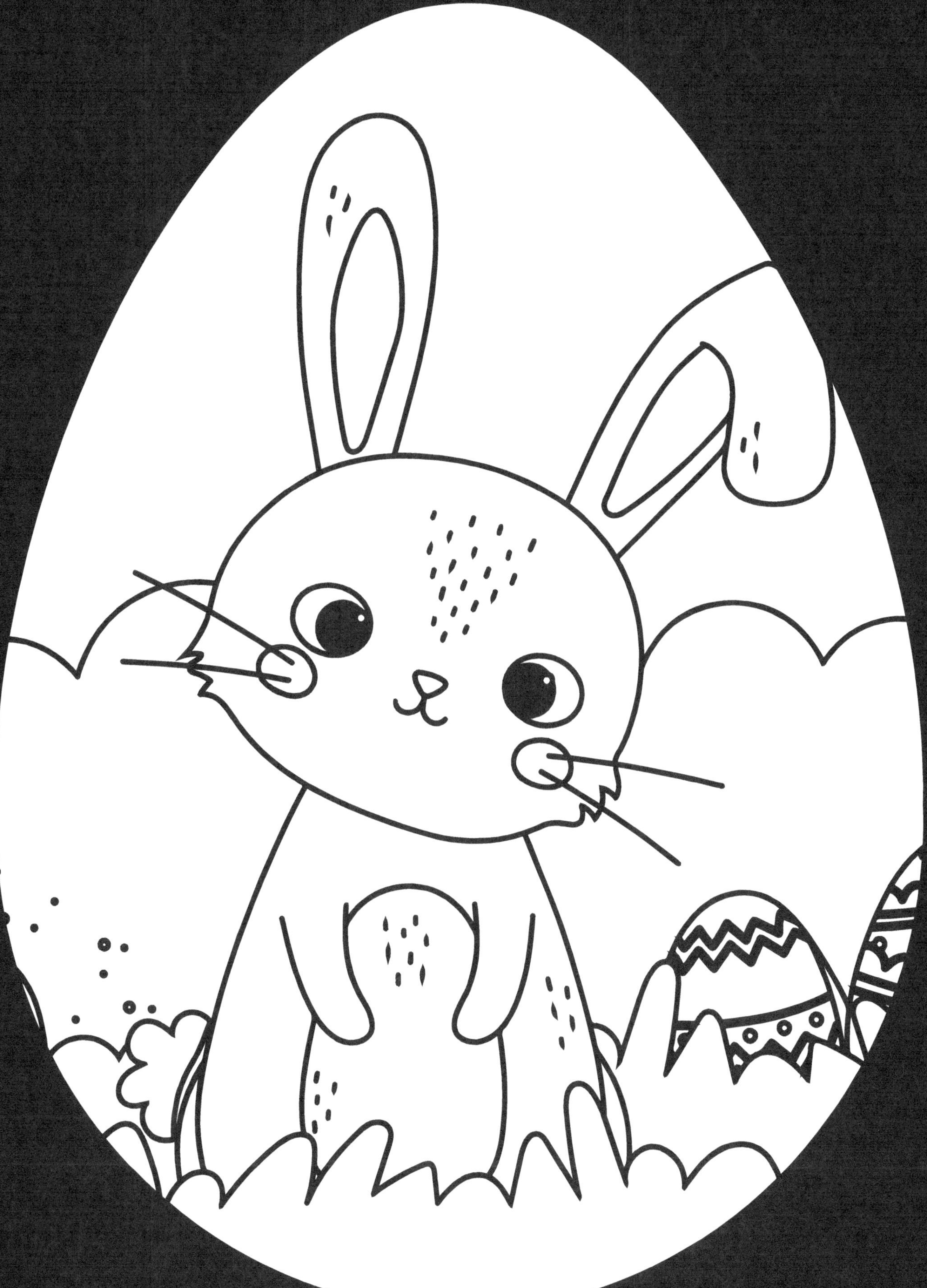

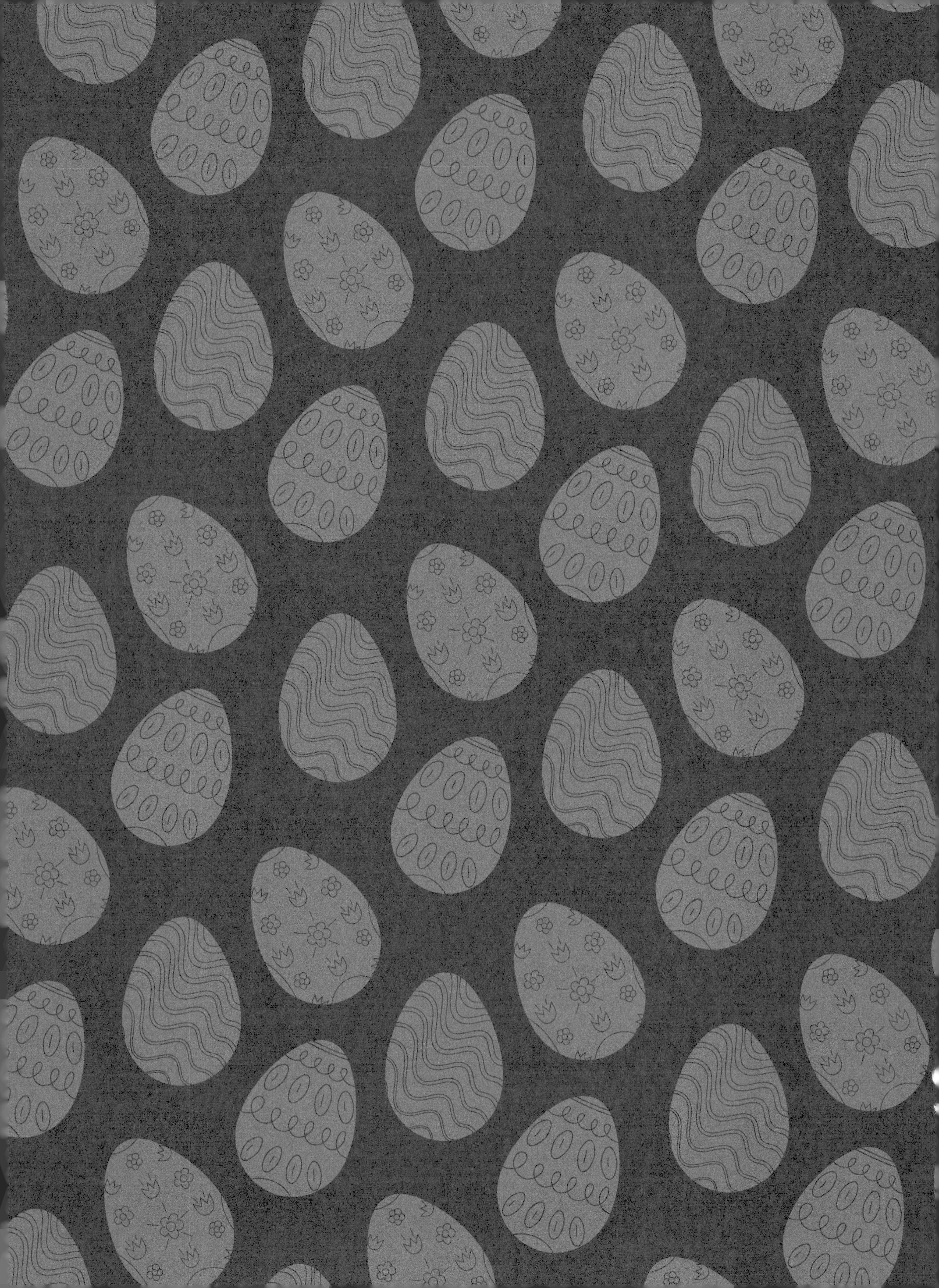

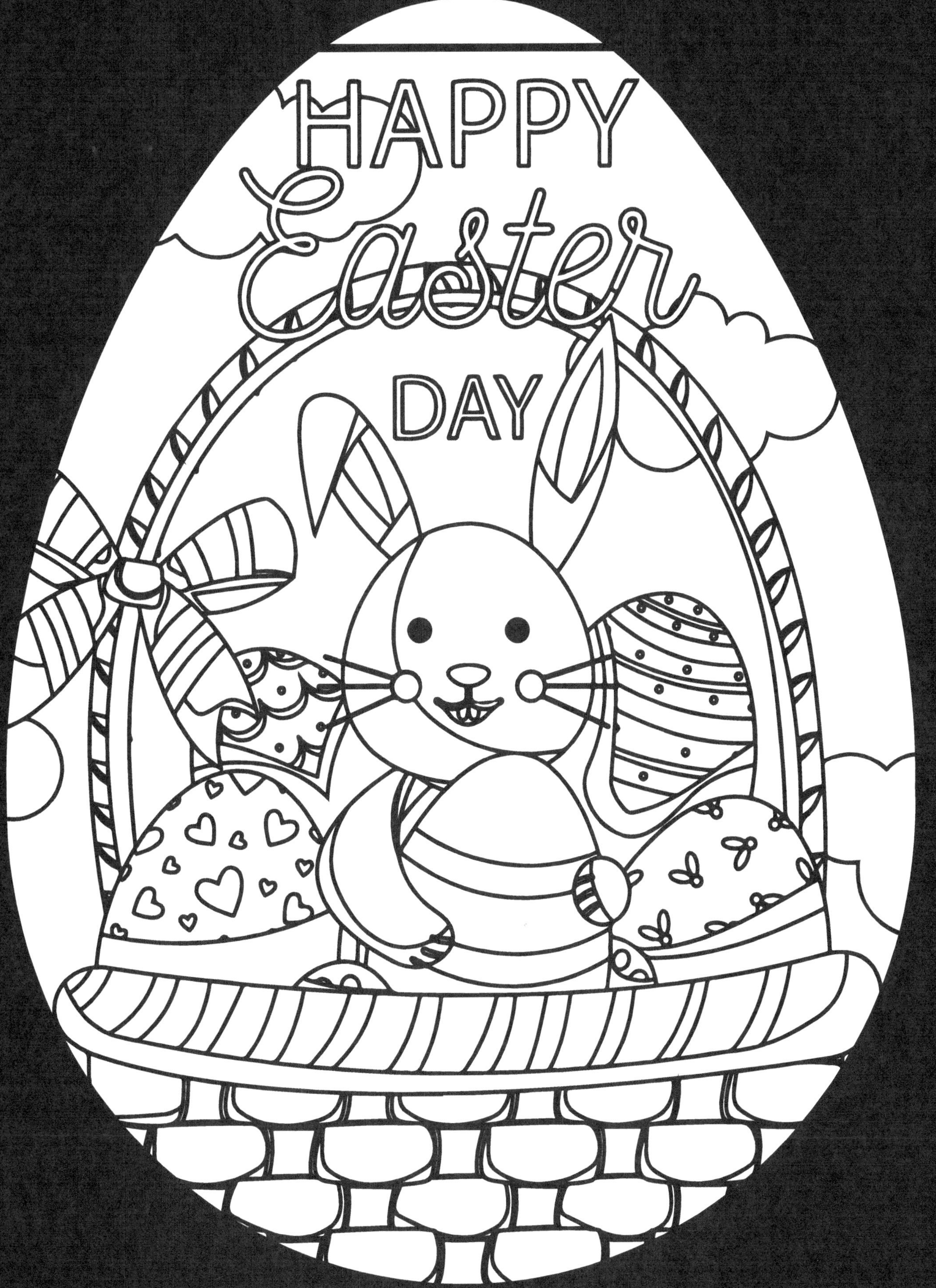
HAPPY
Easter
DAY

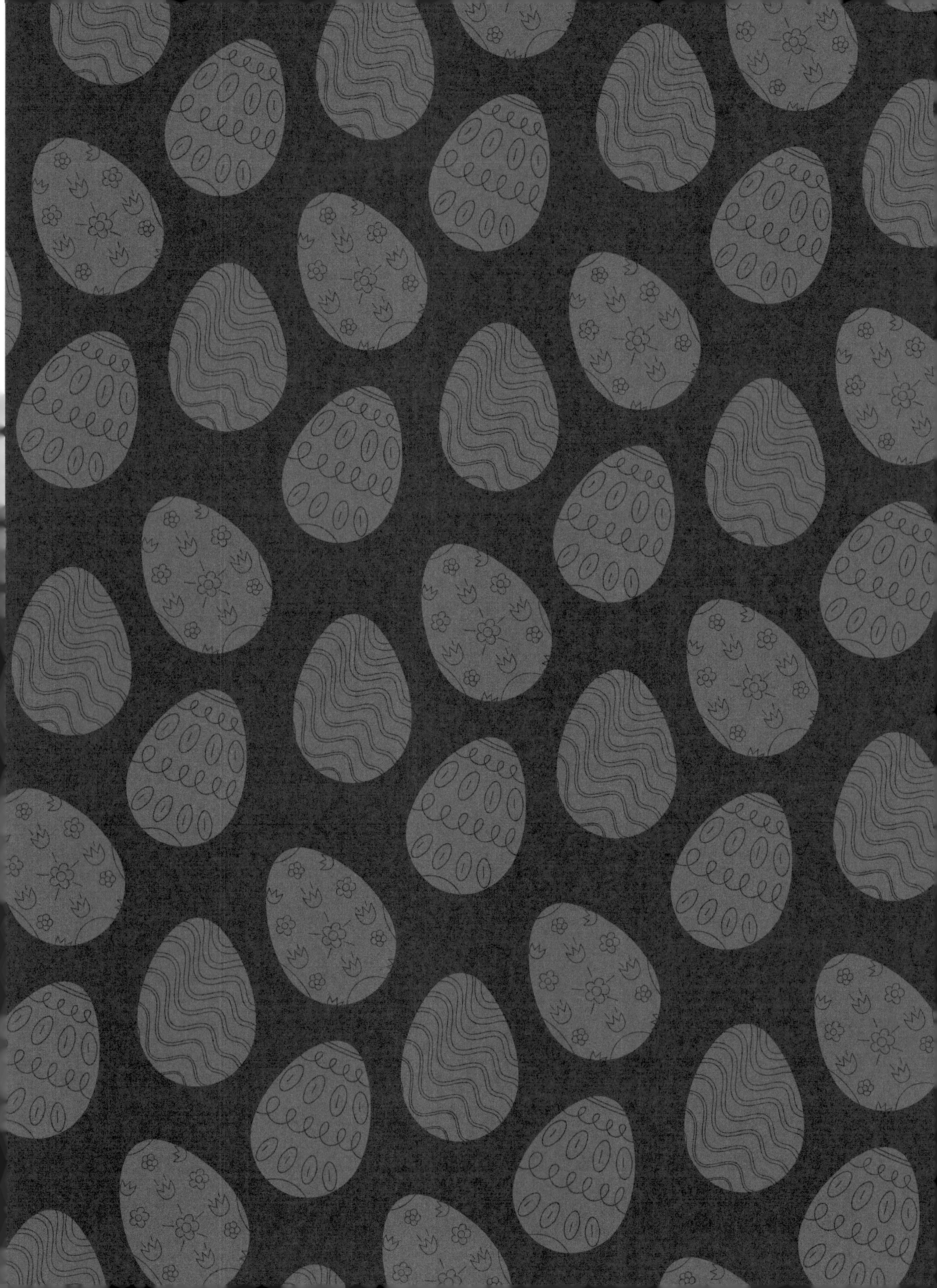

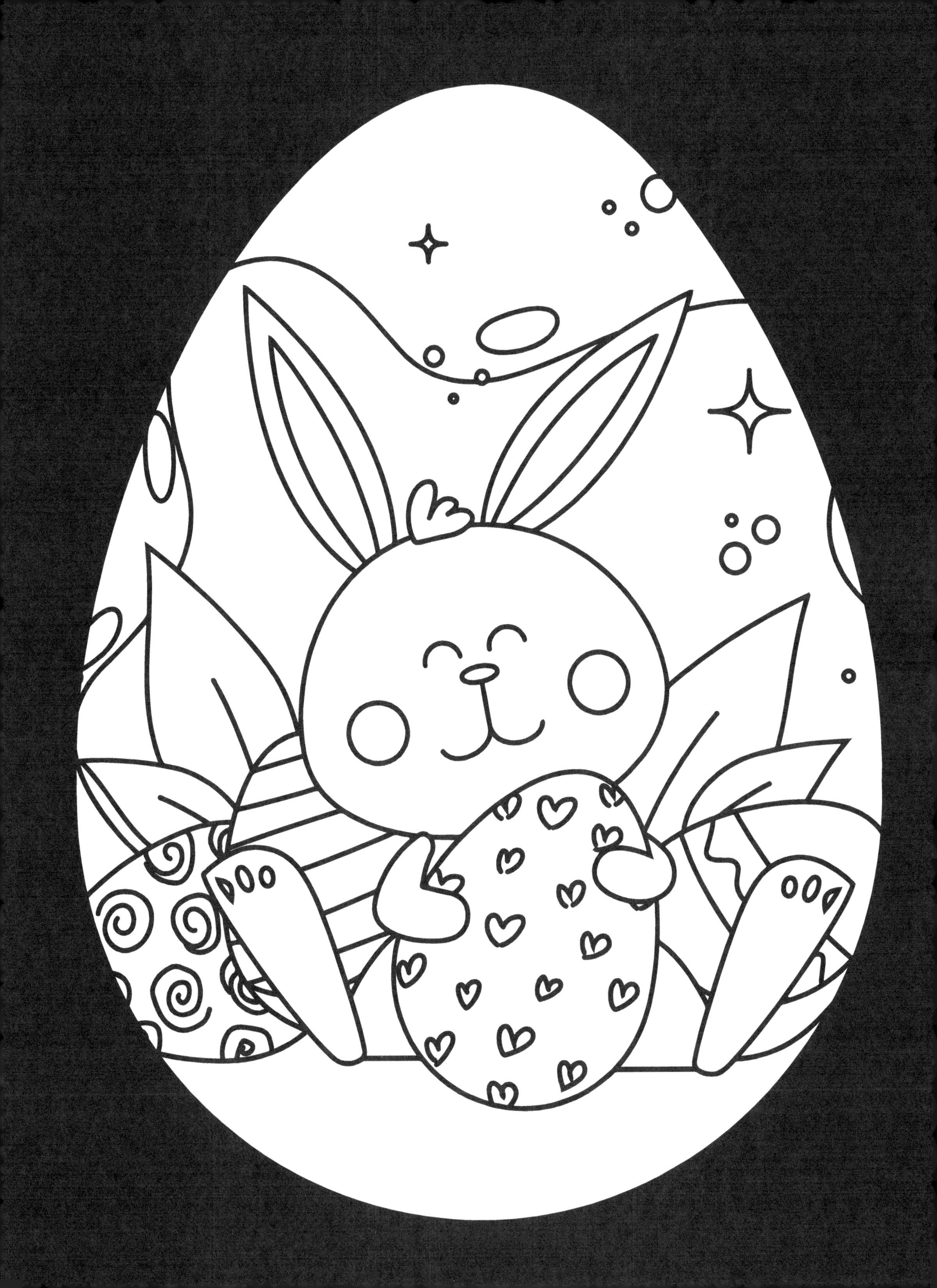

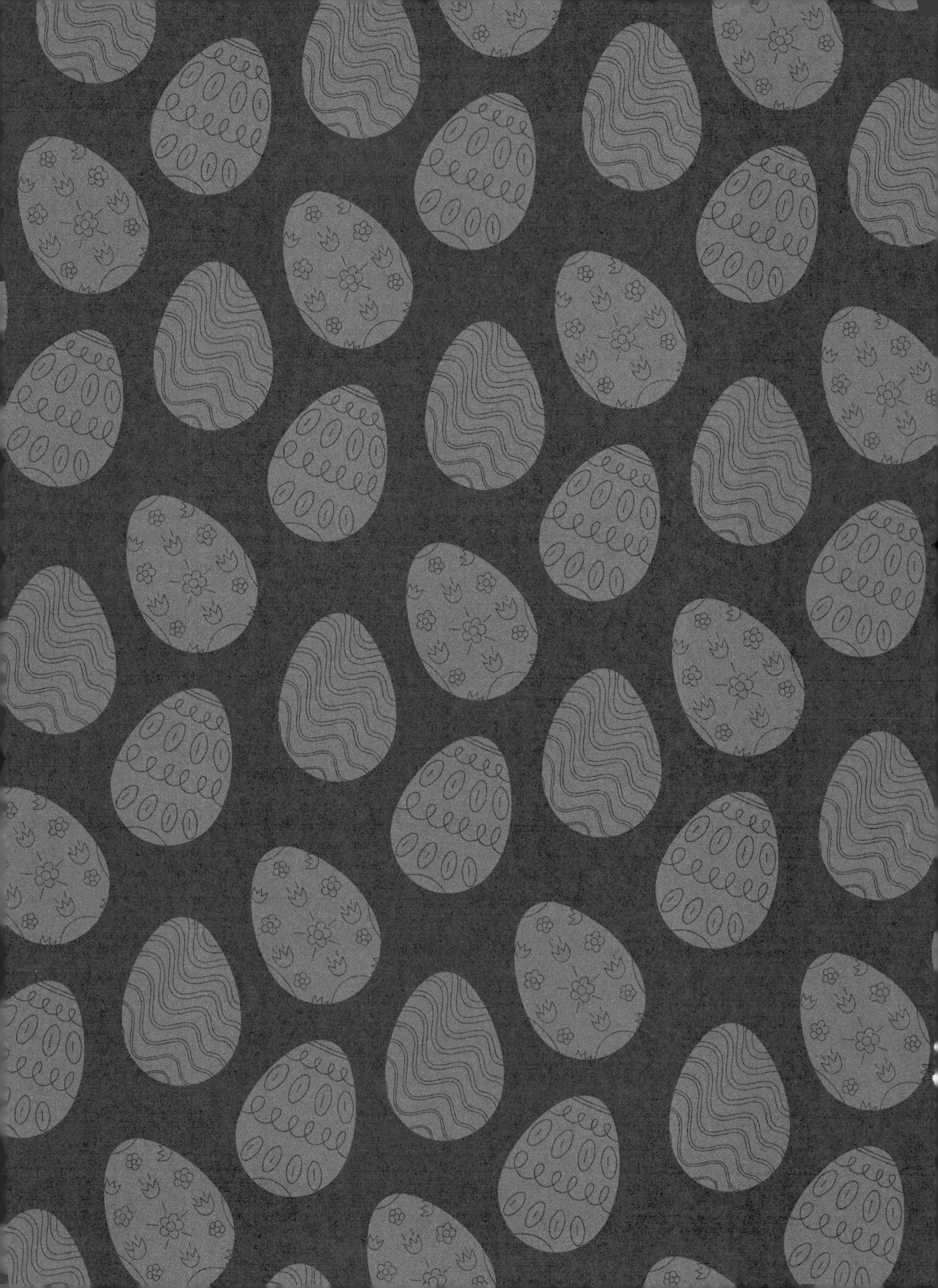

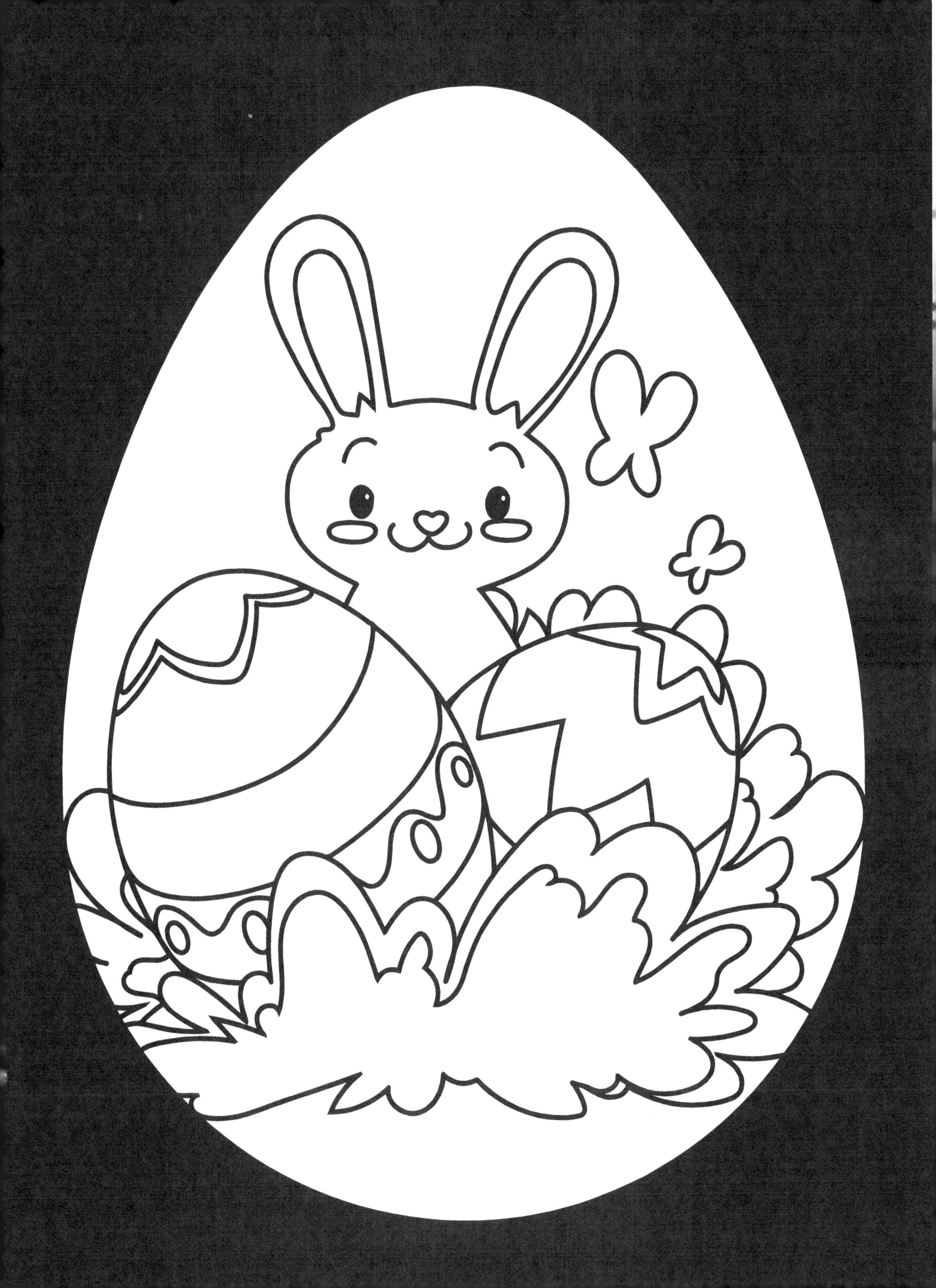

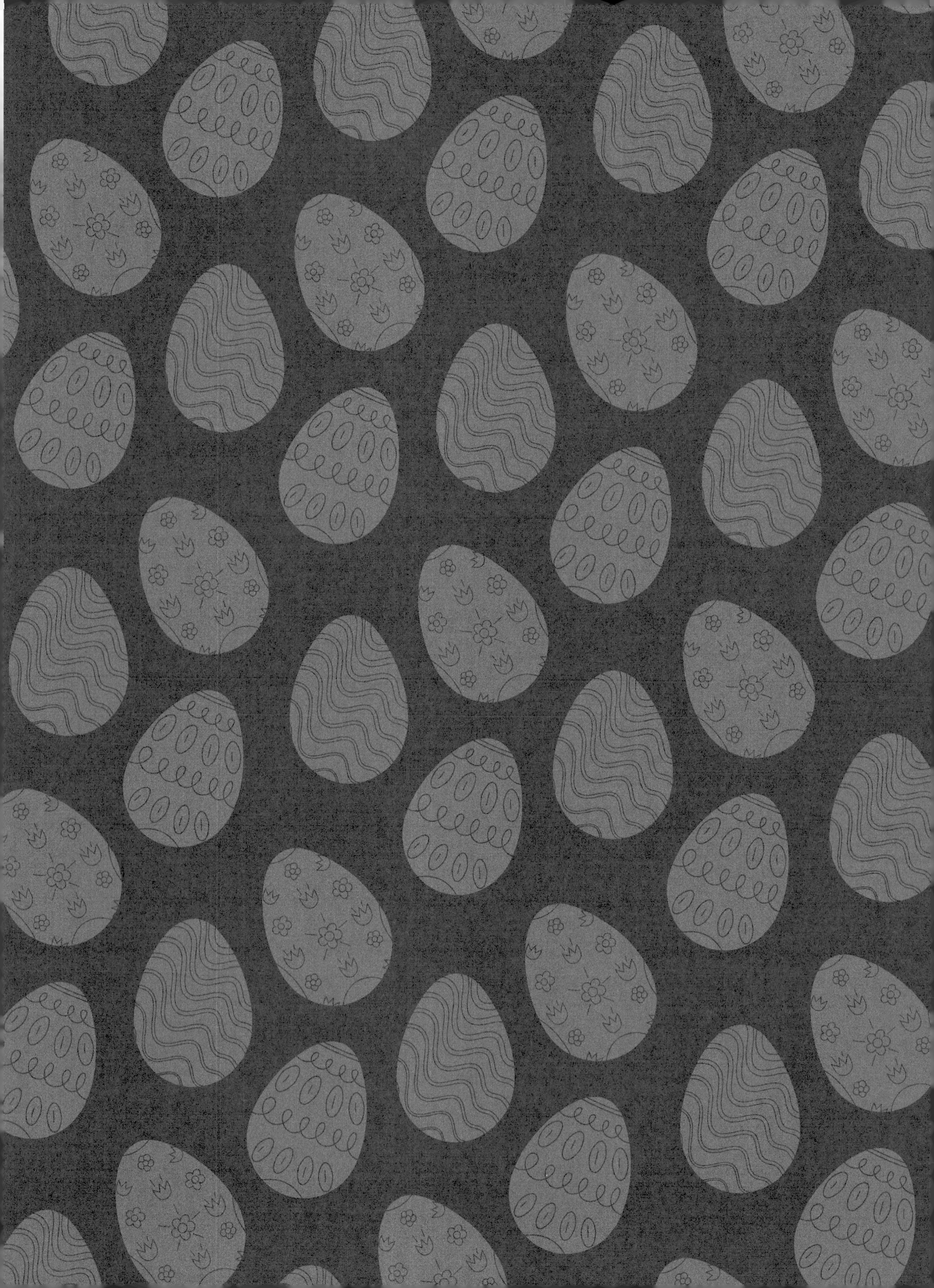

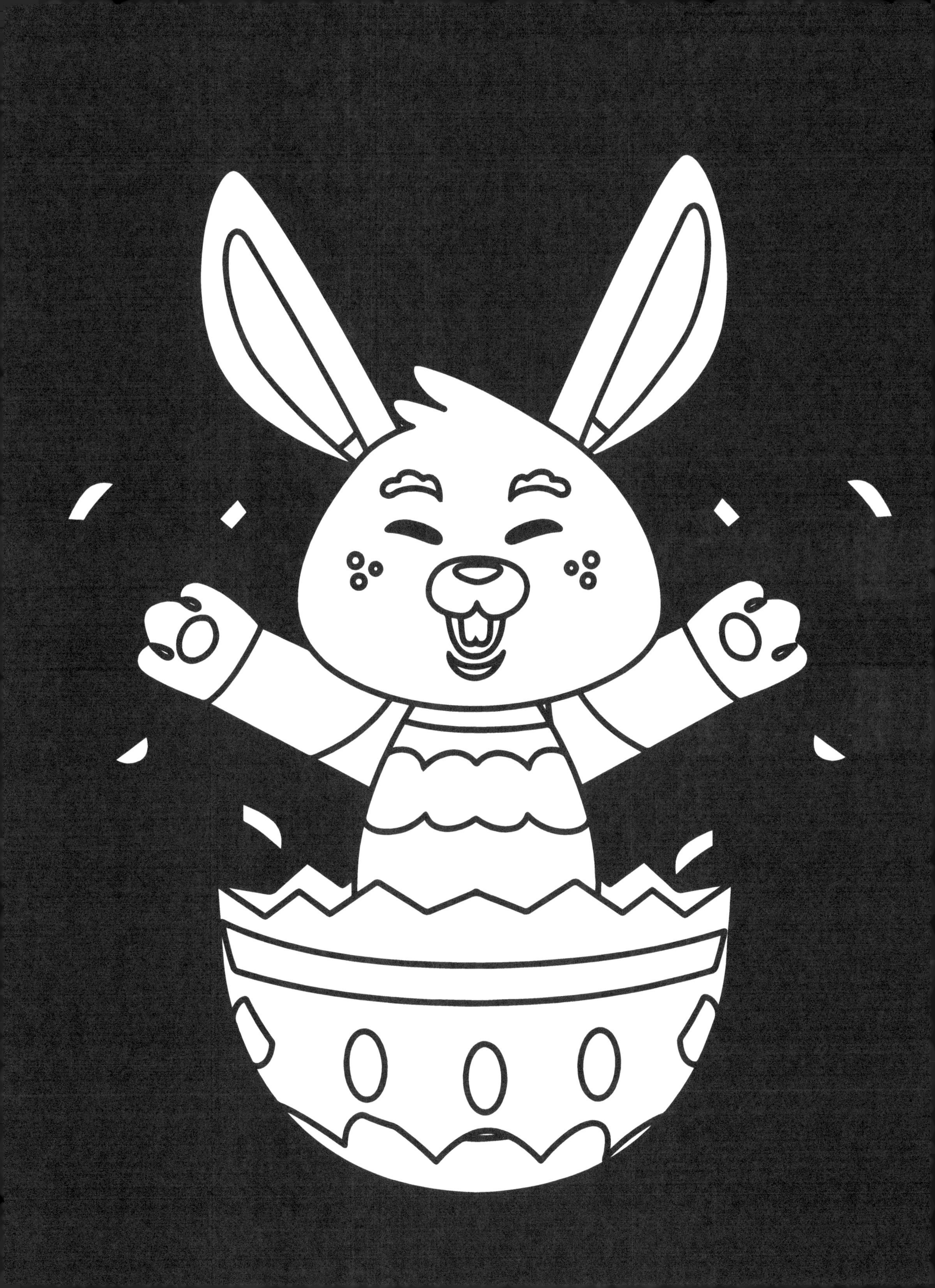

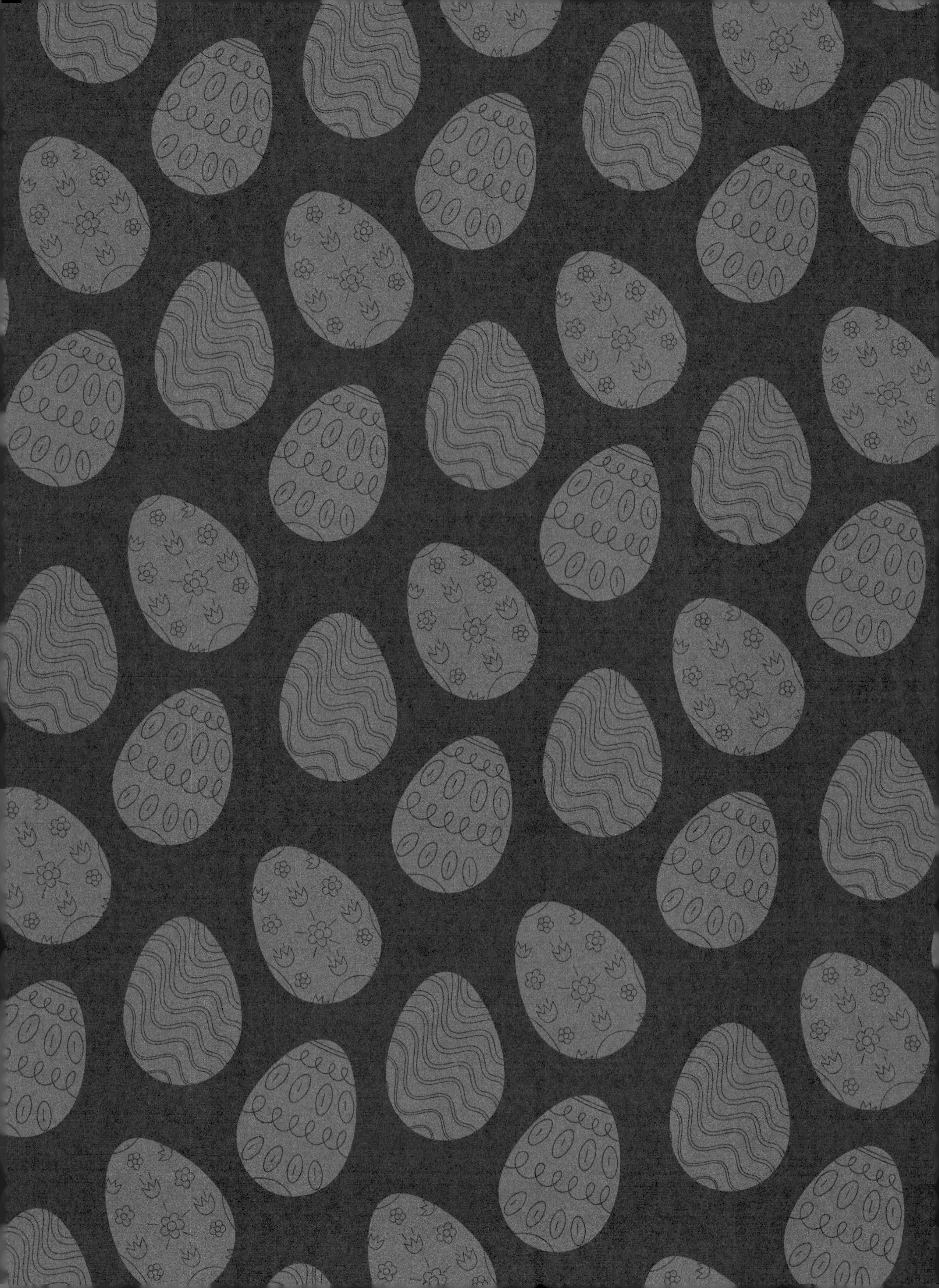

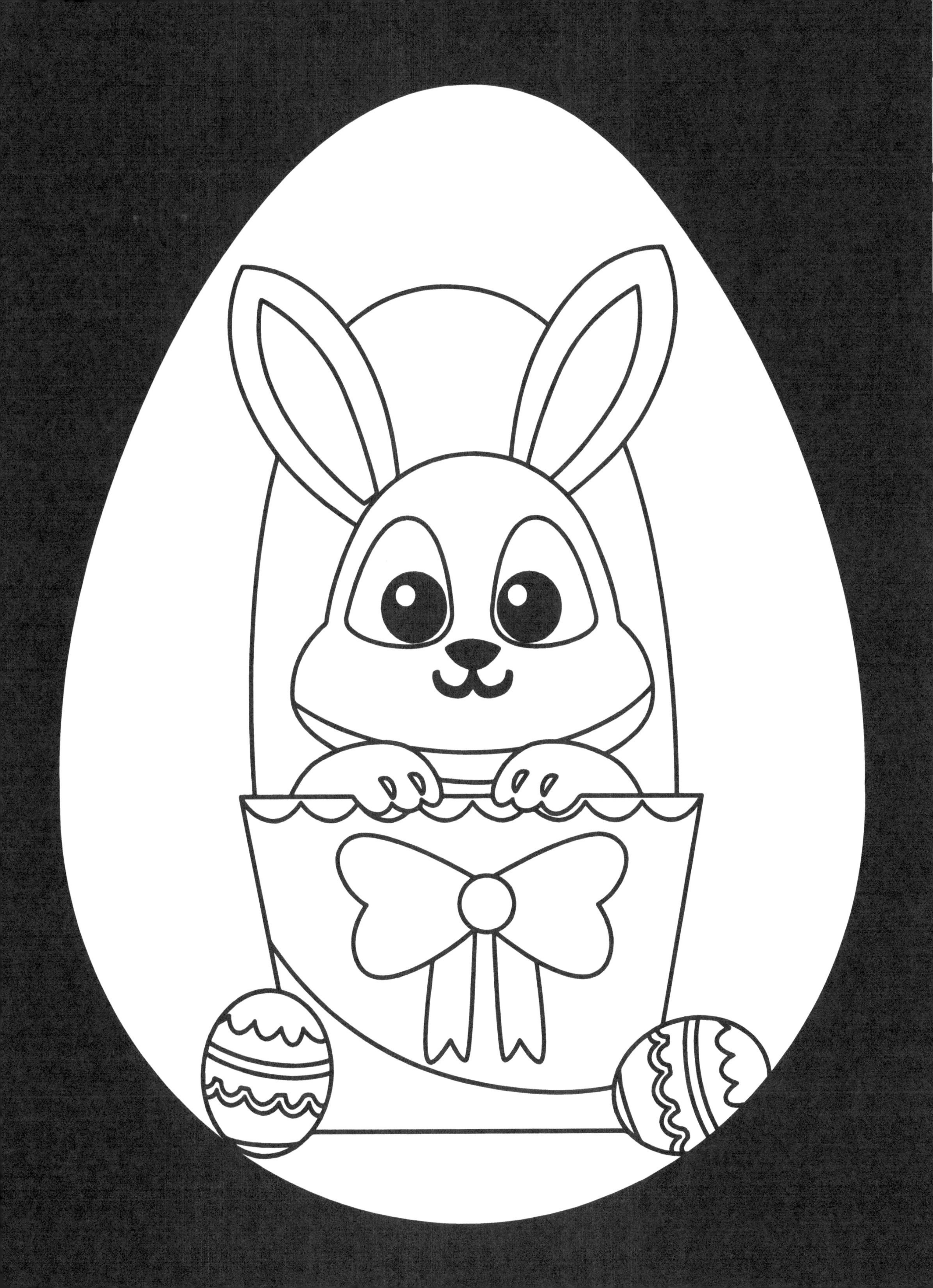

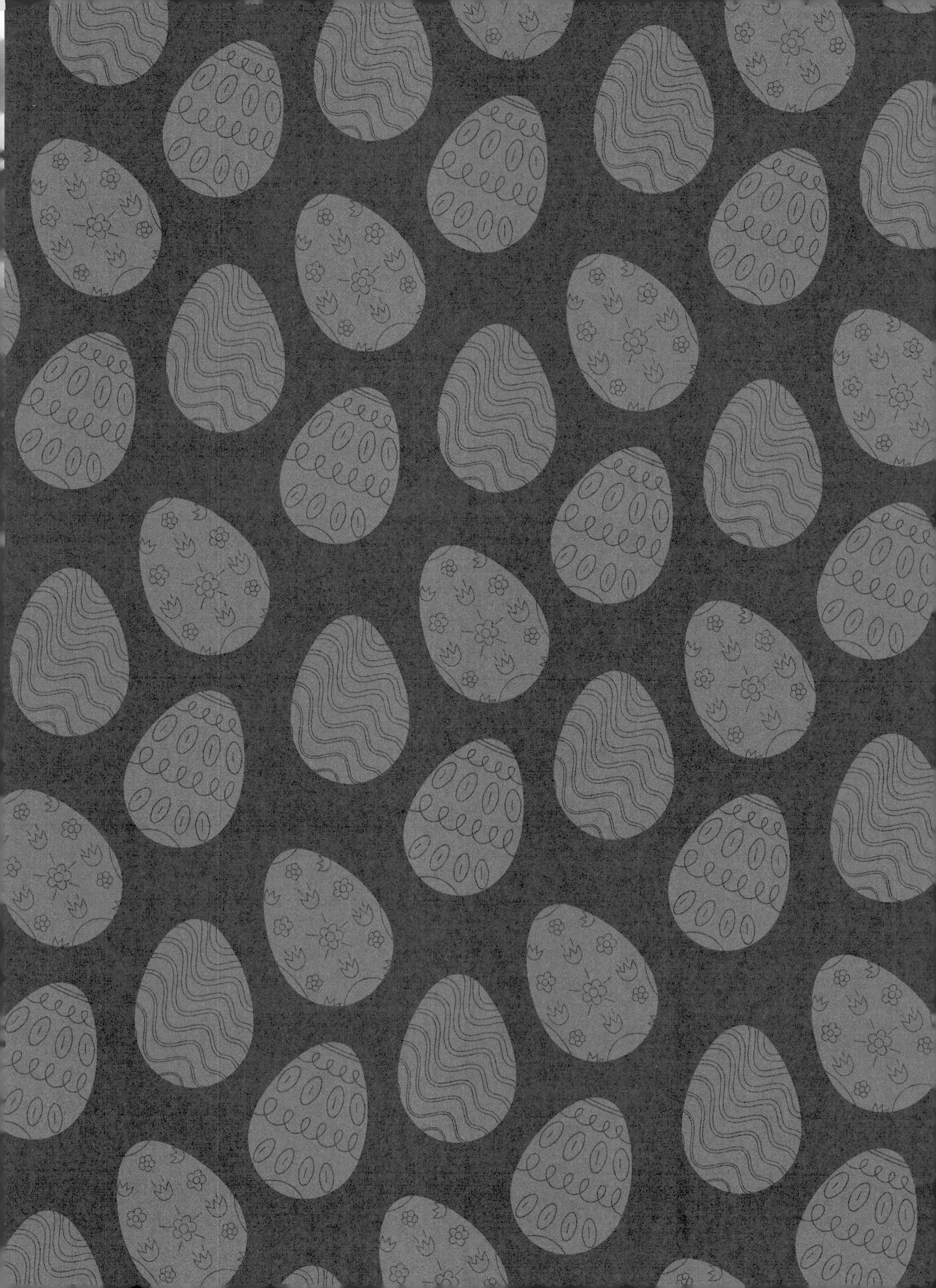

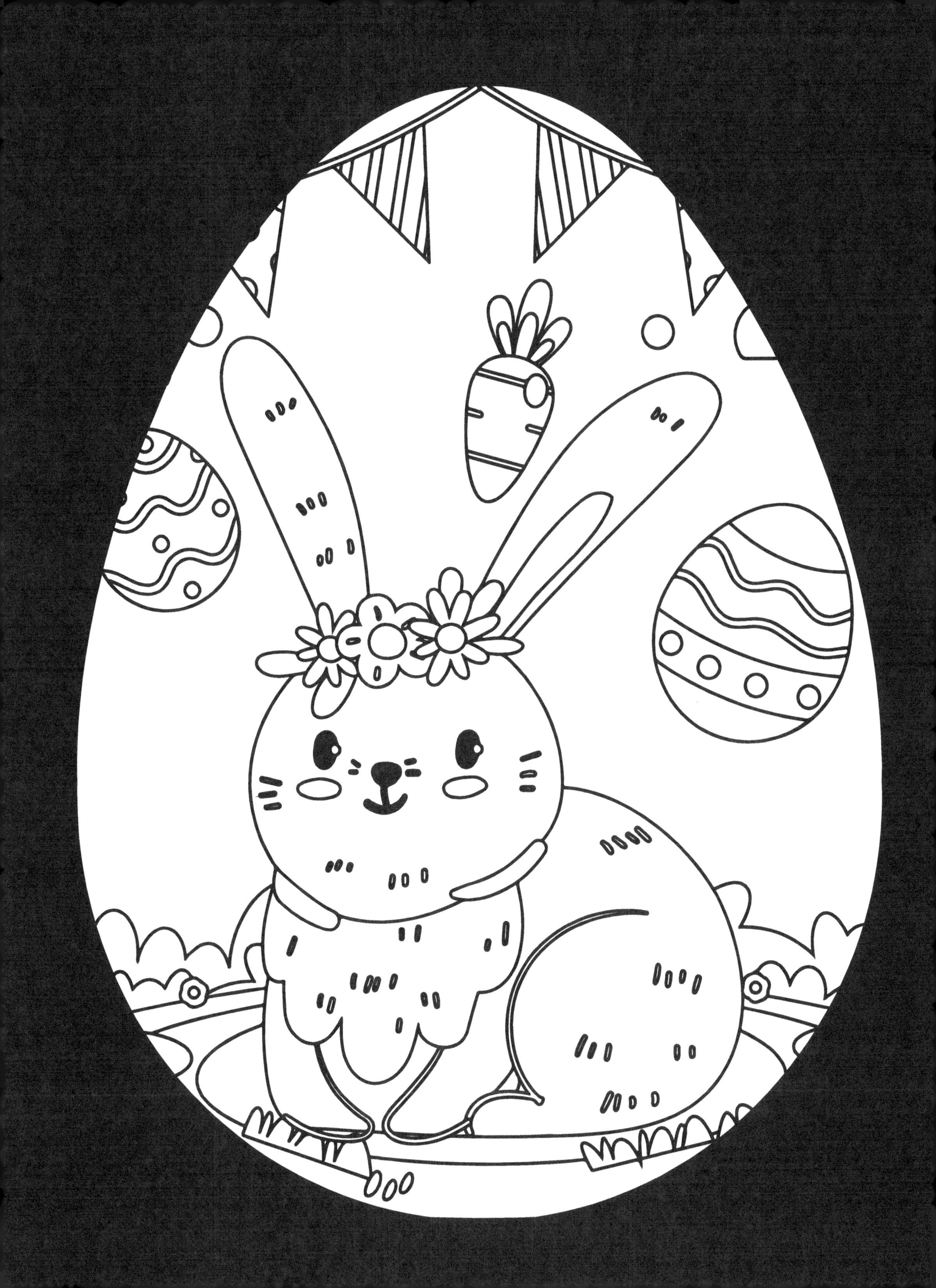

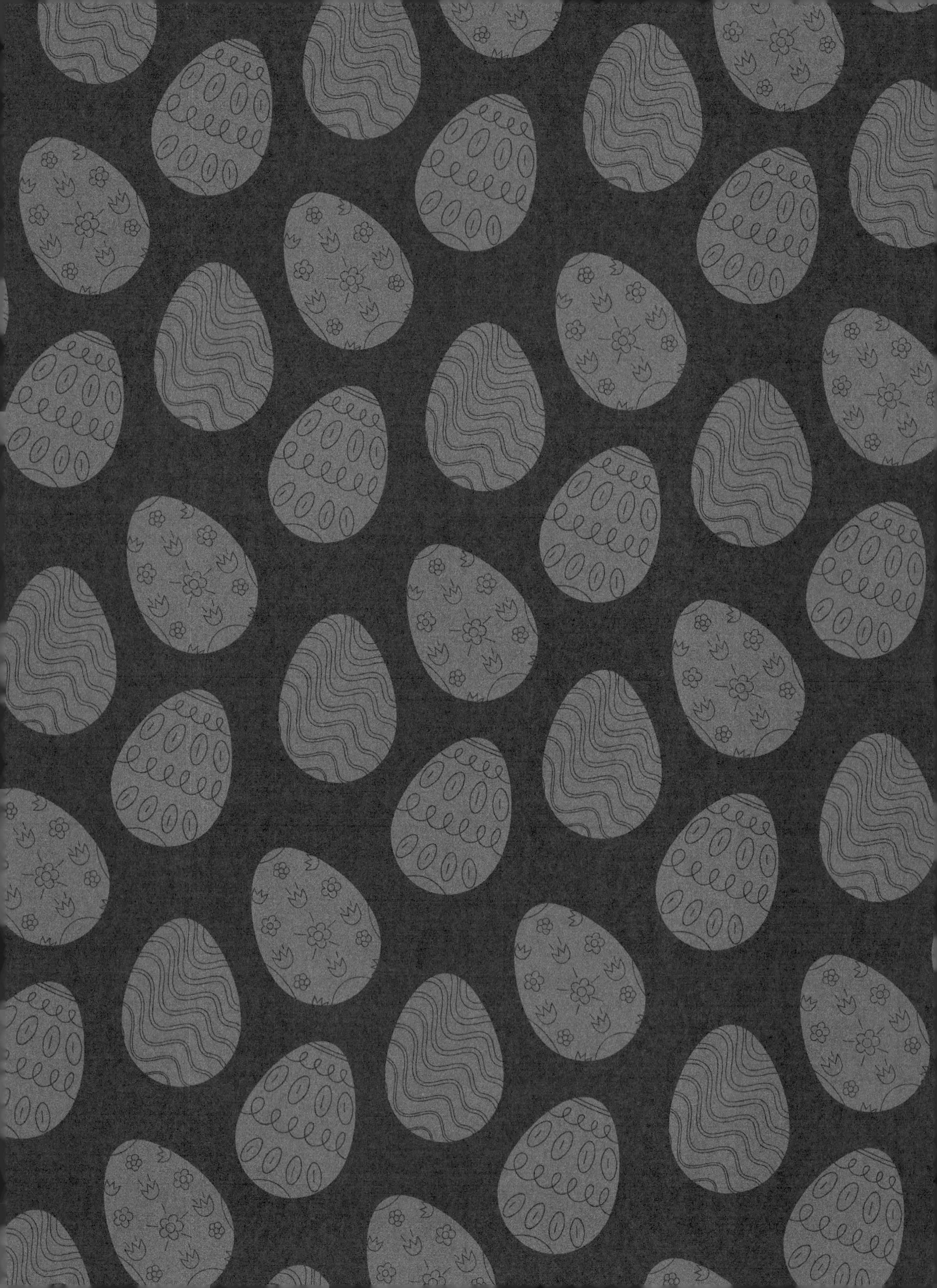

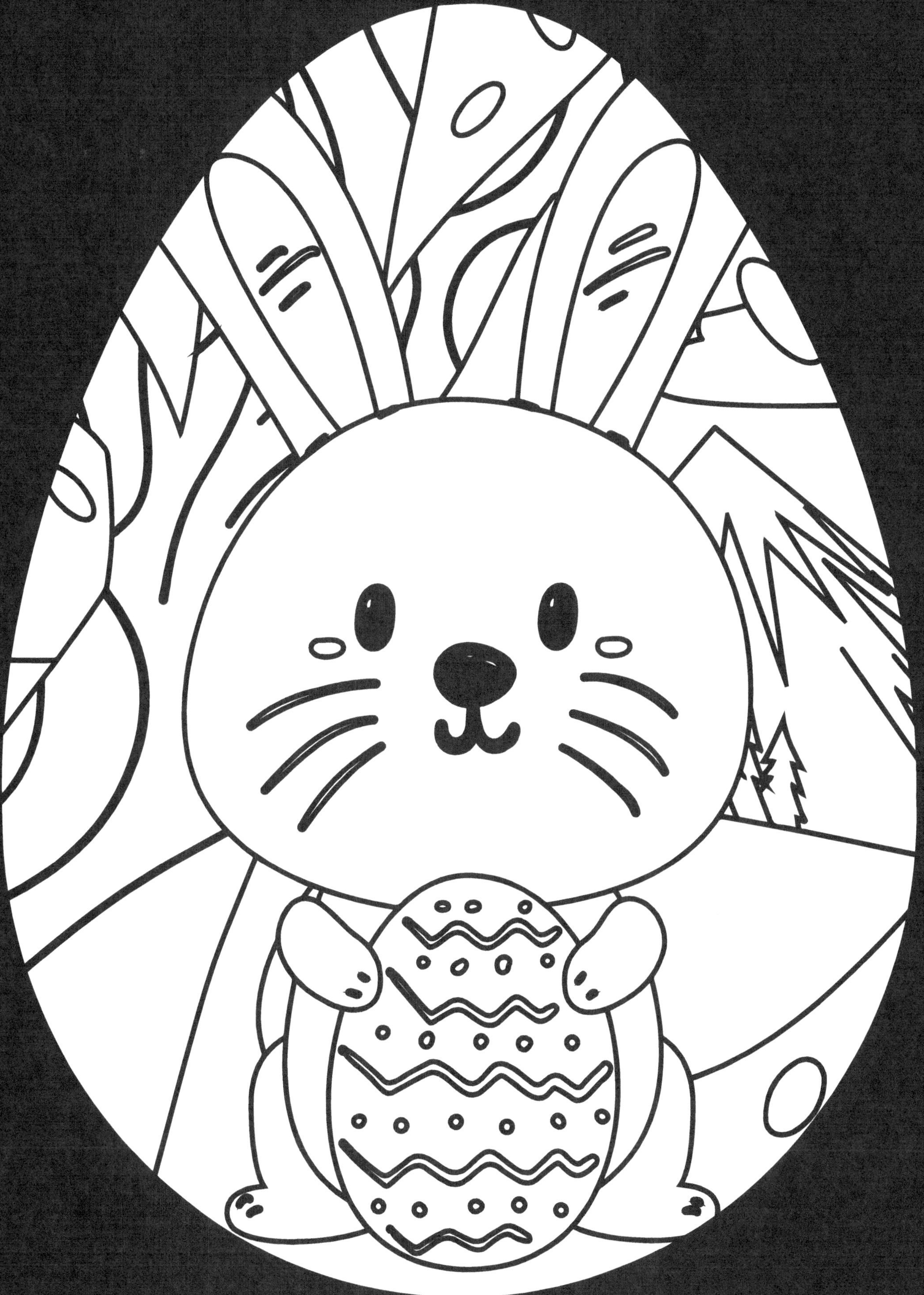

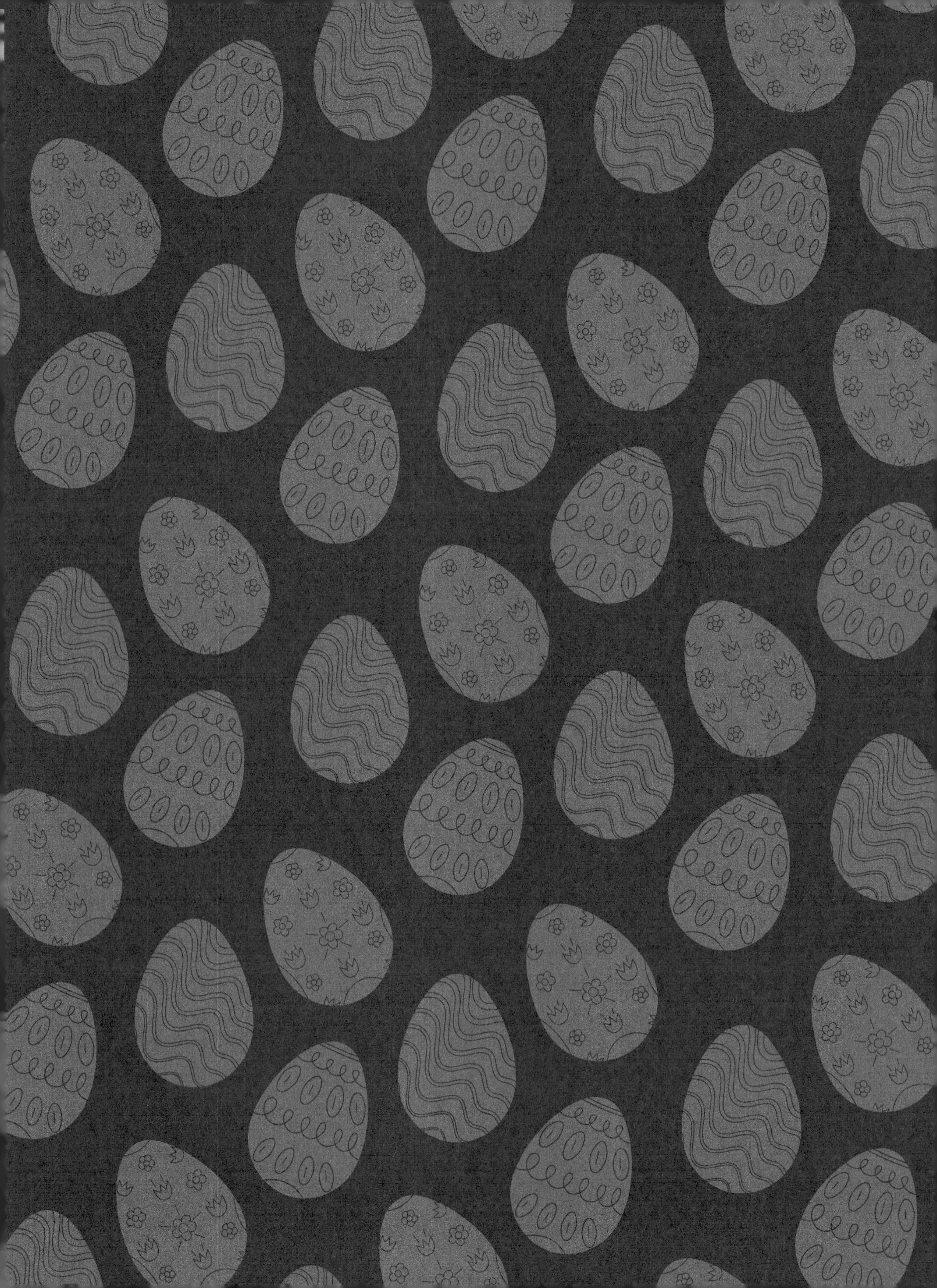

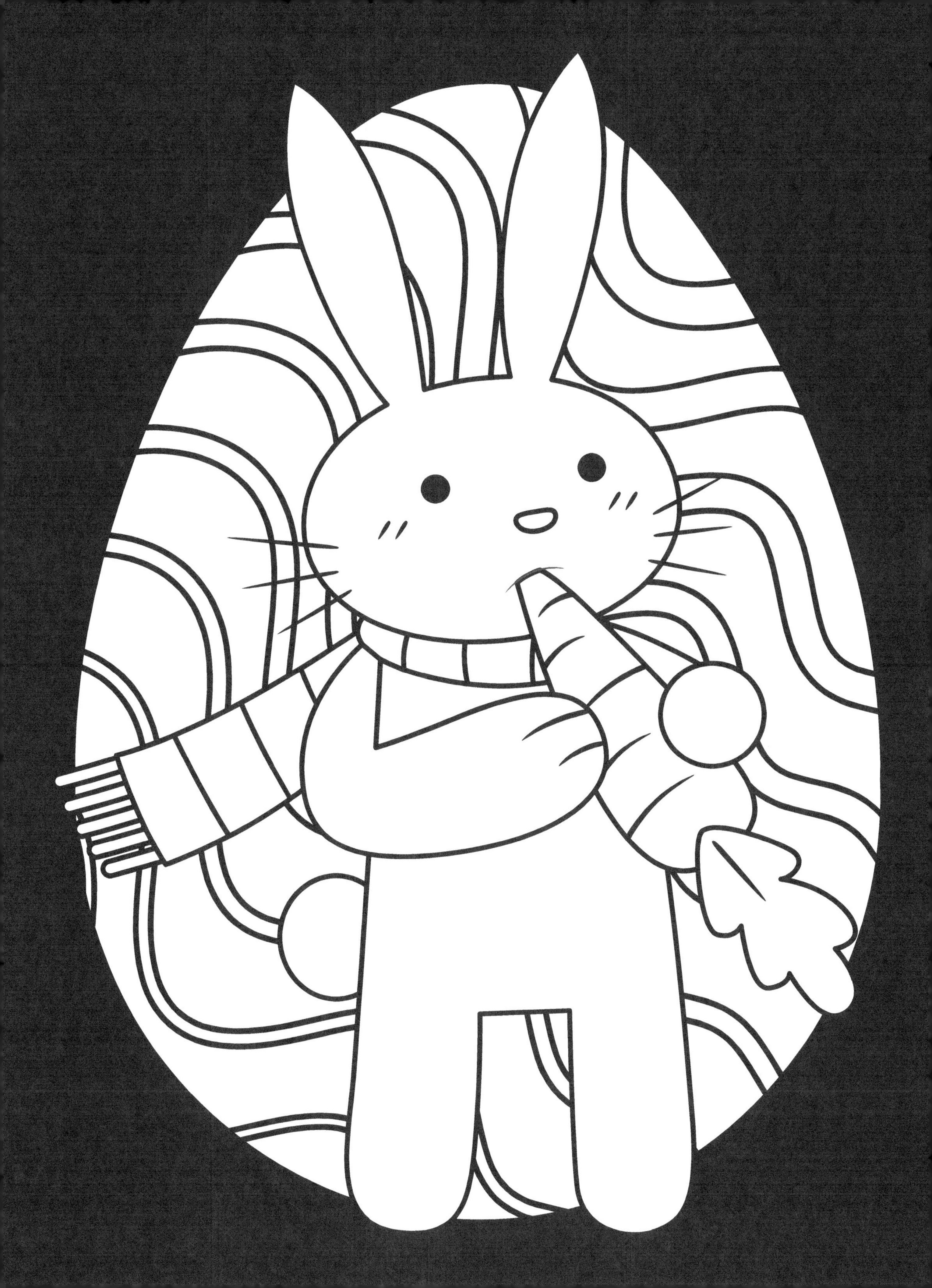

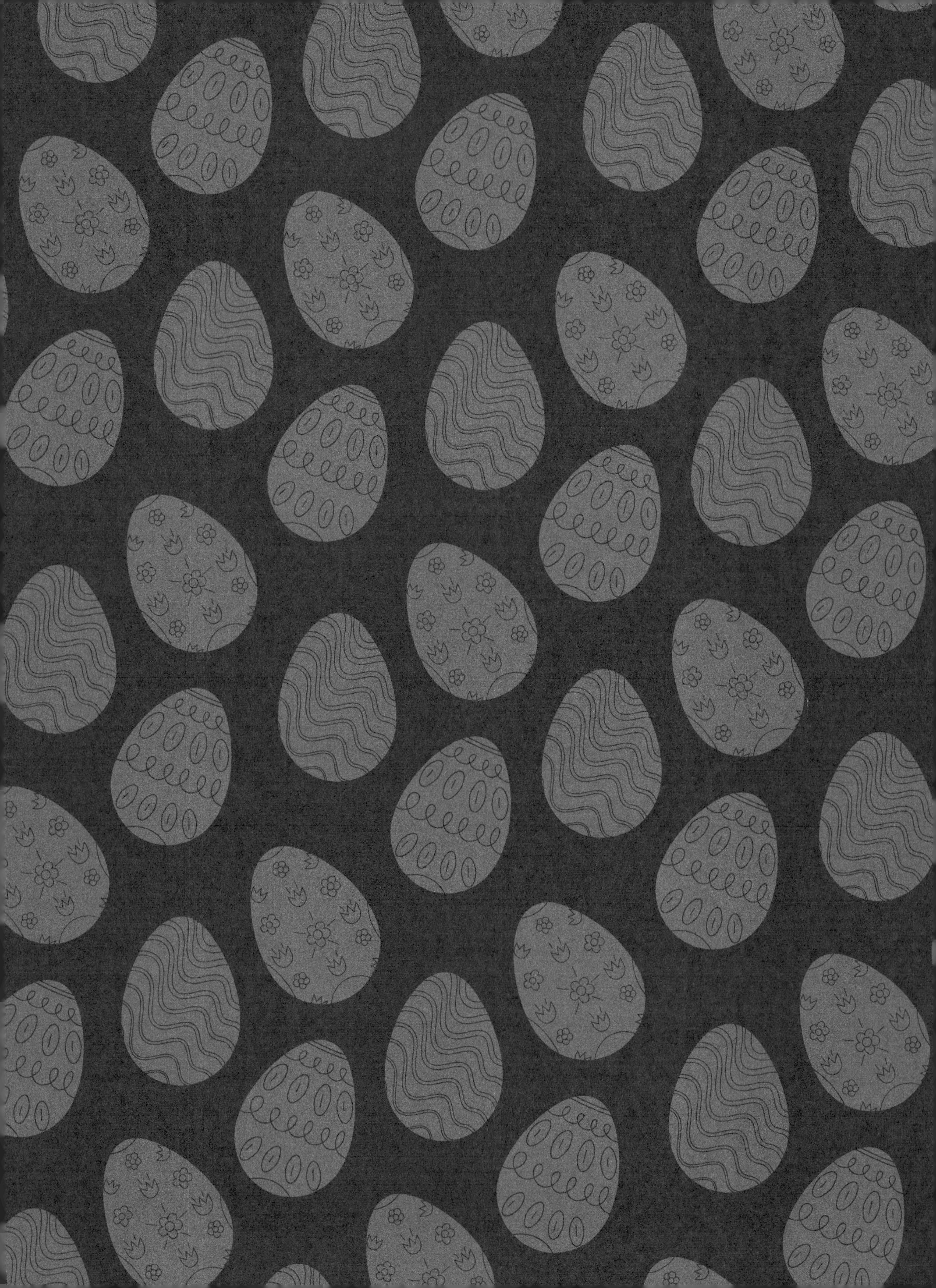

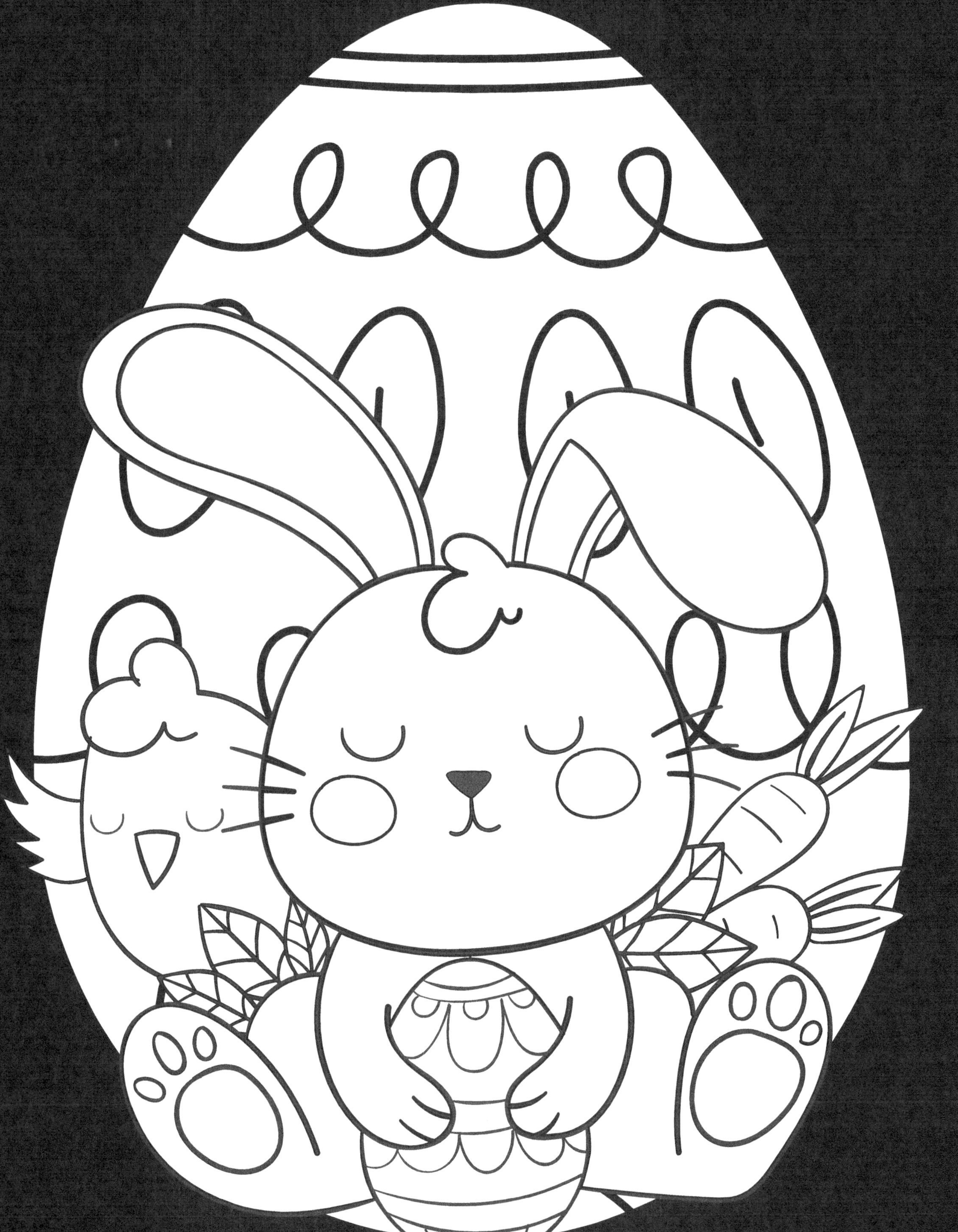

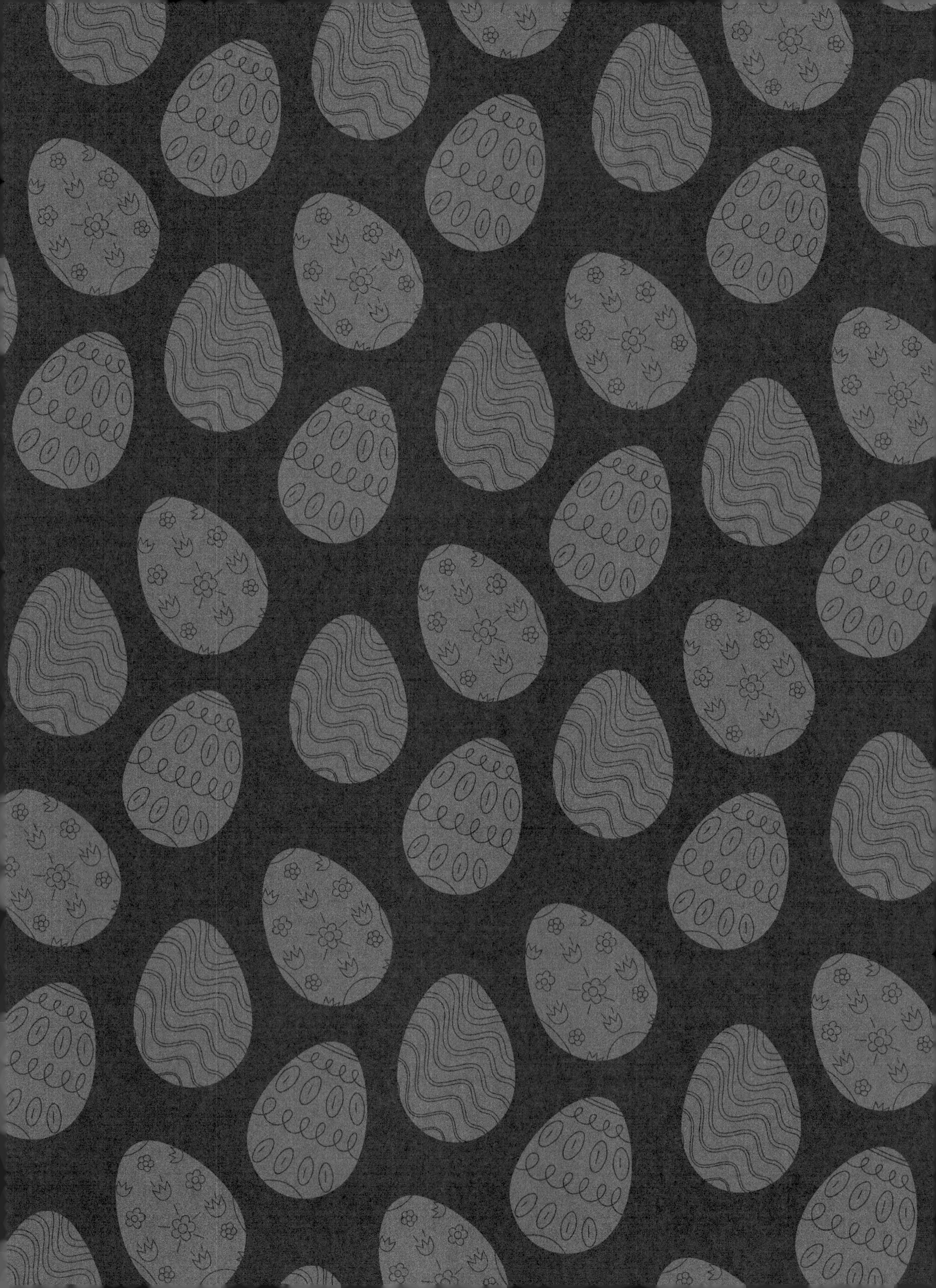

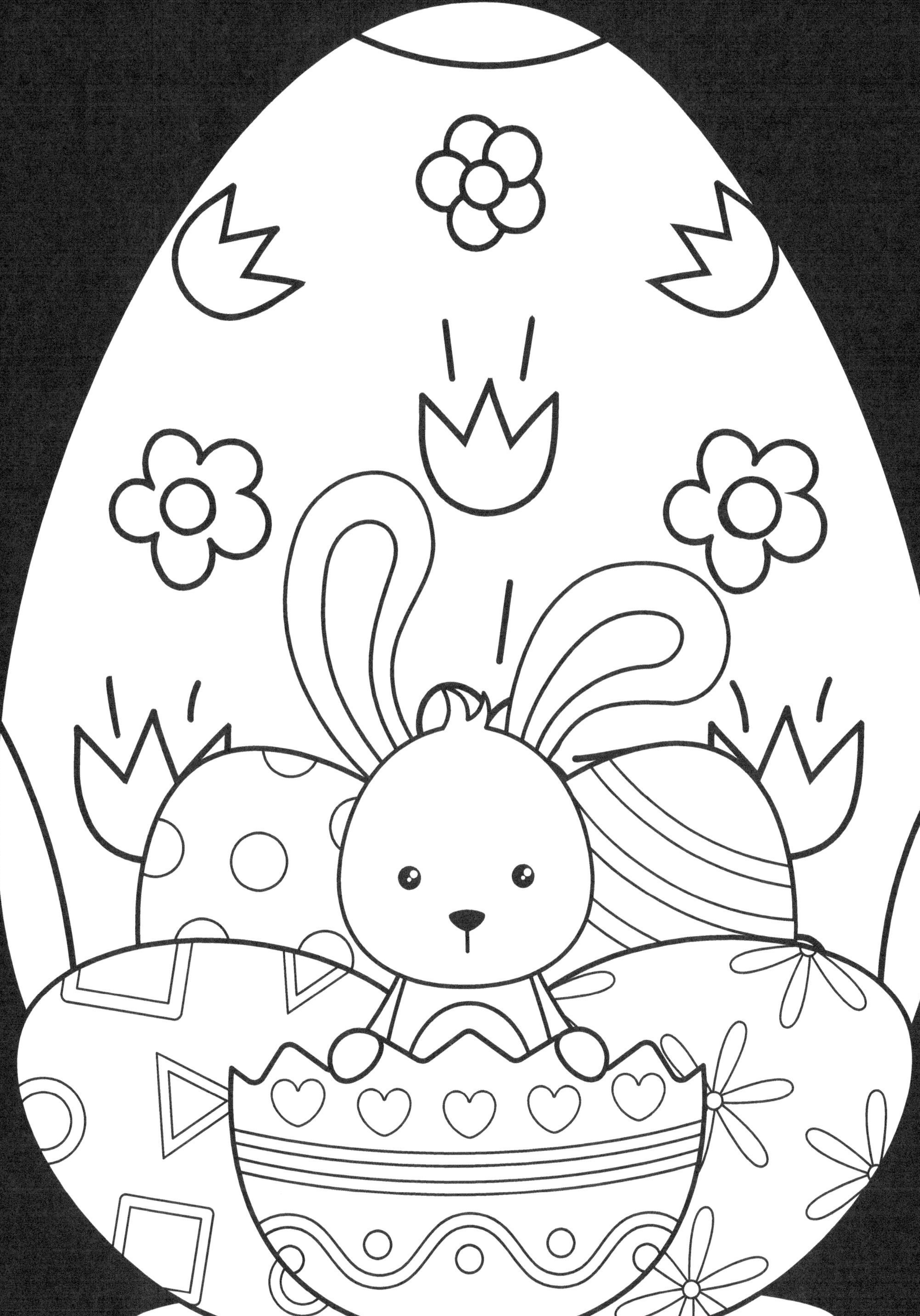

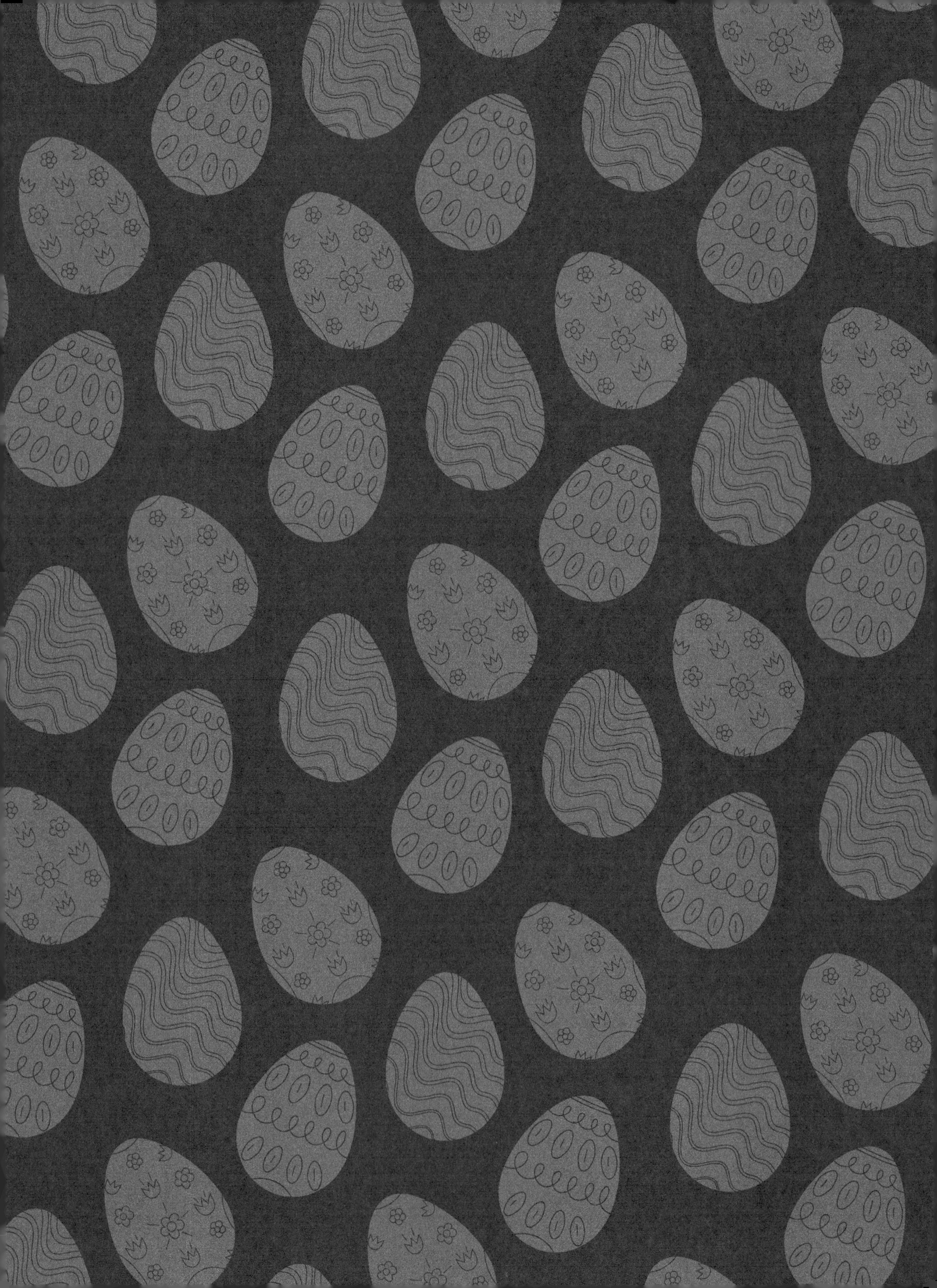

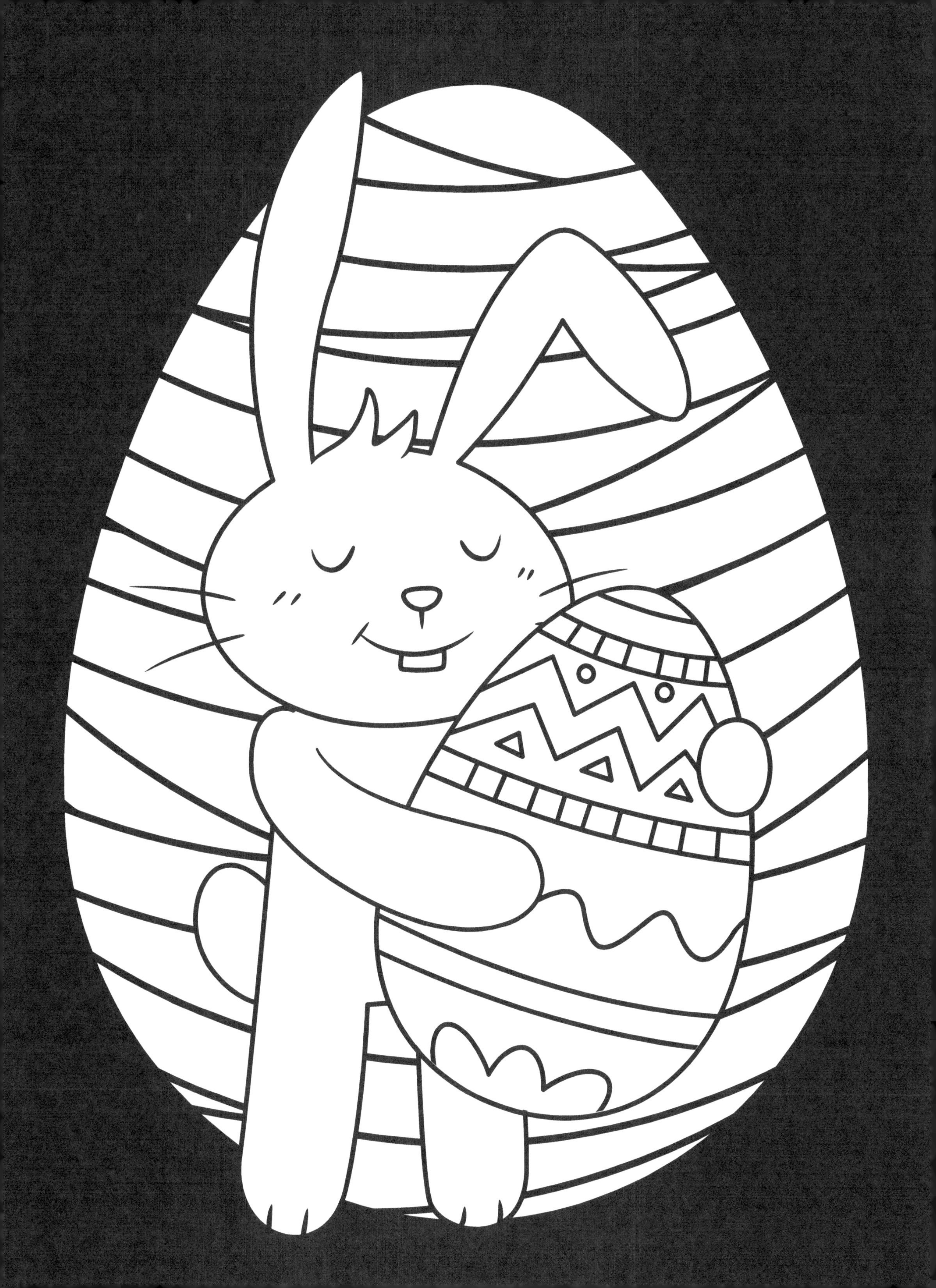

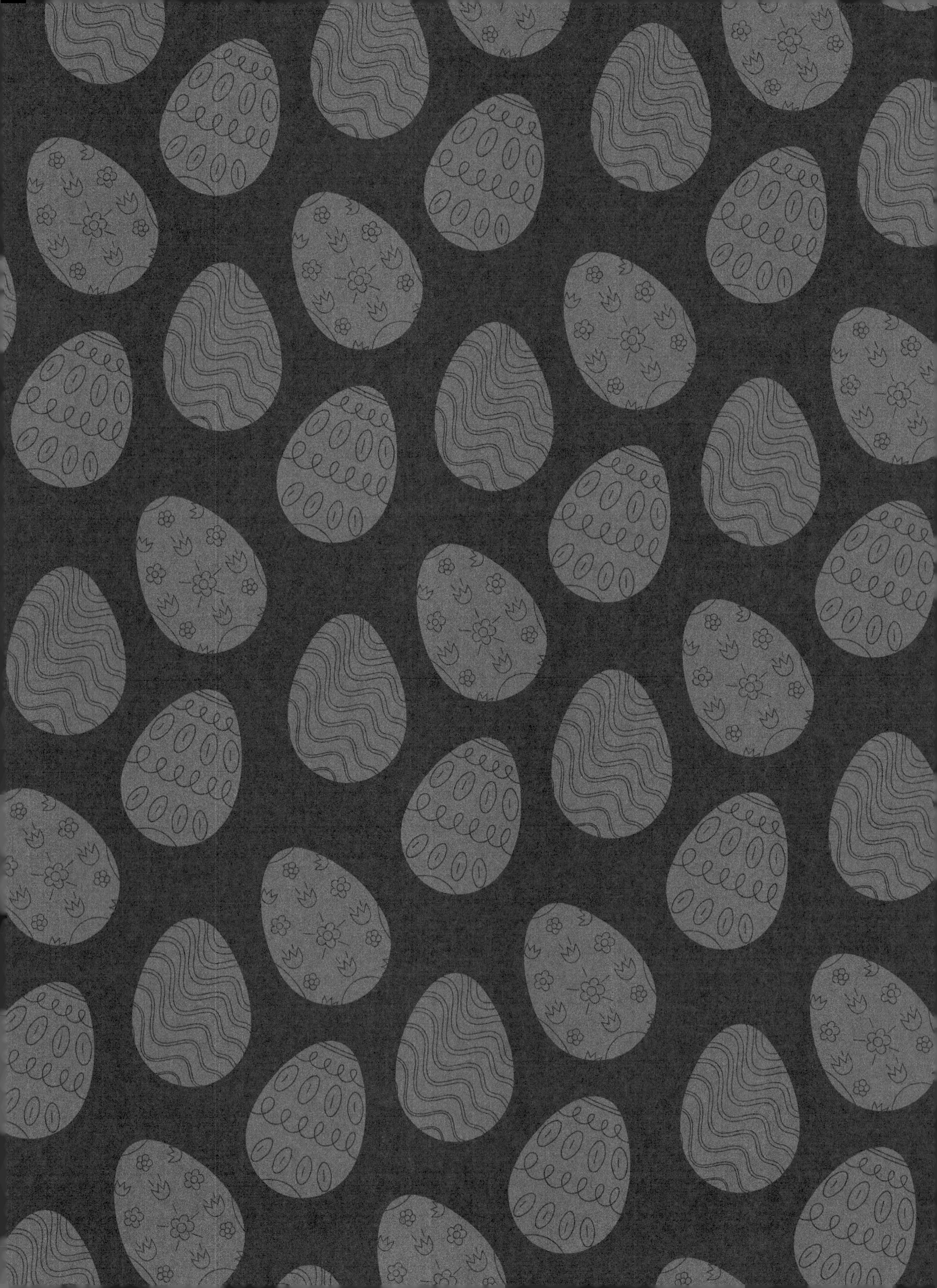

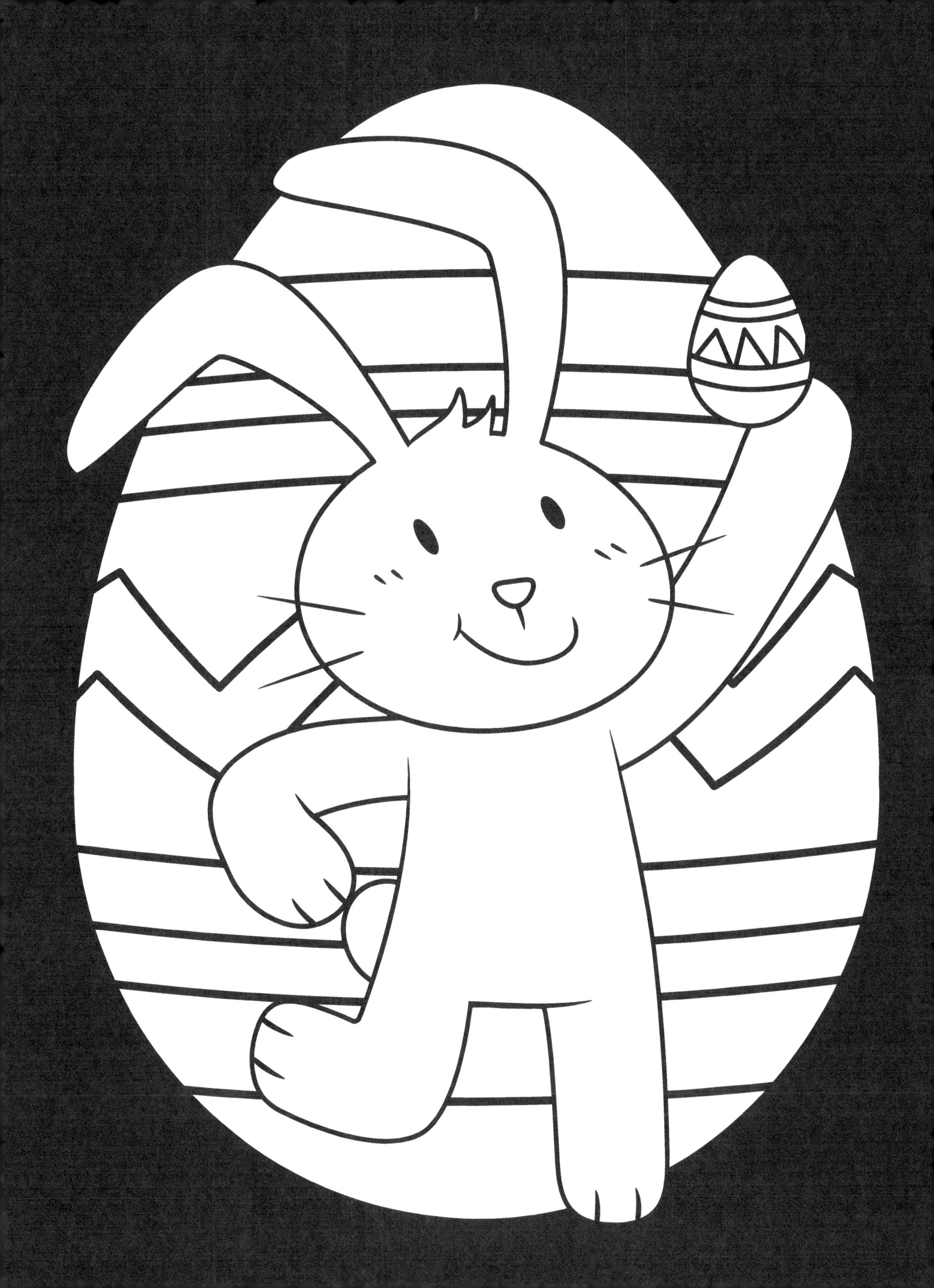

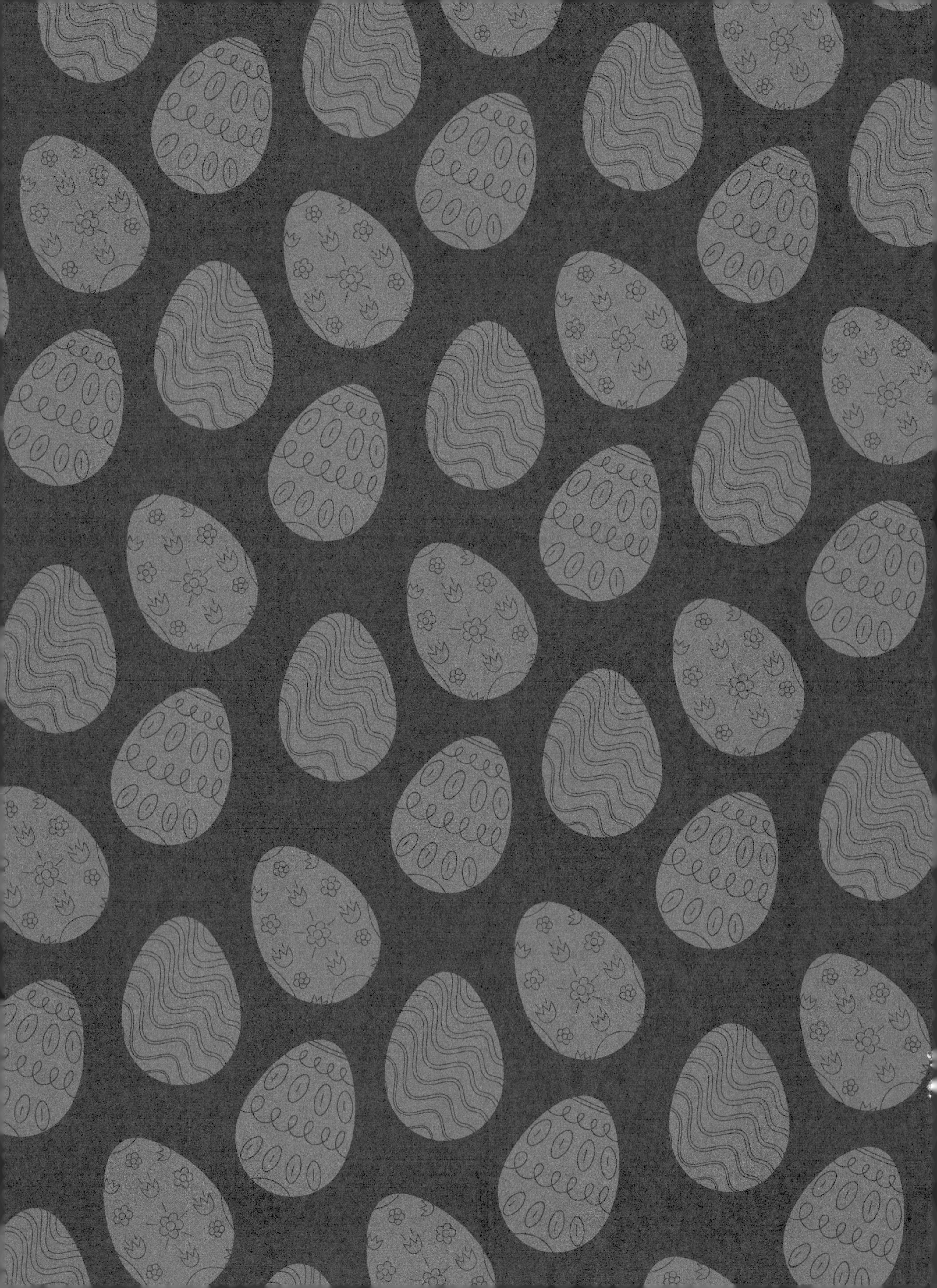

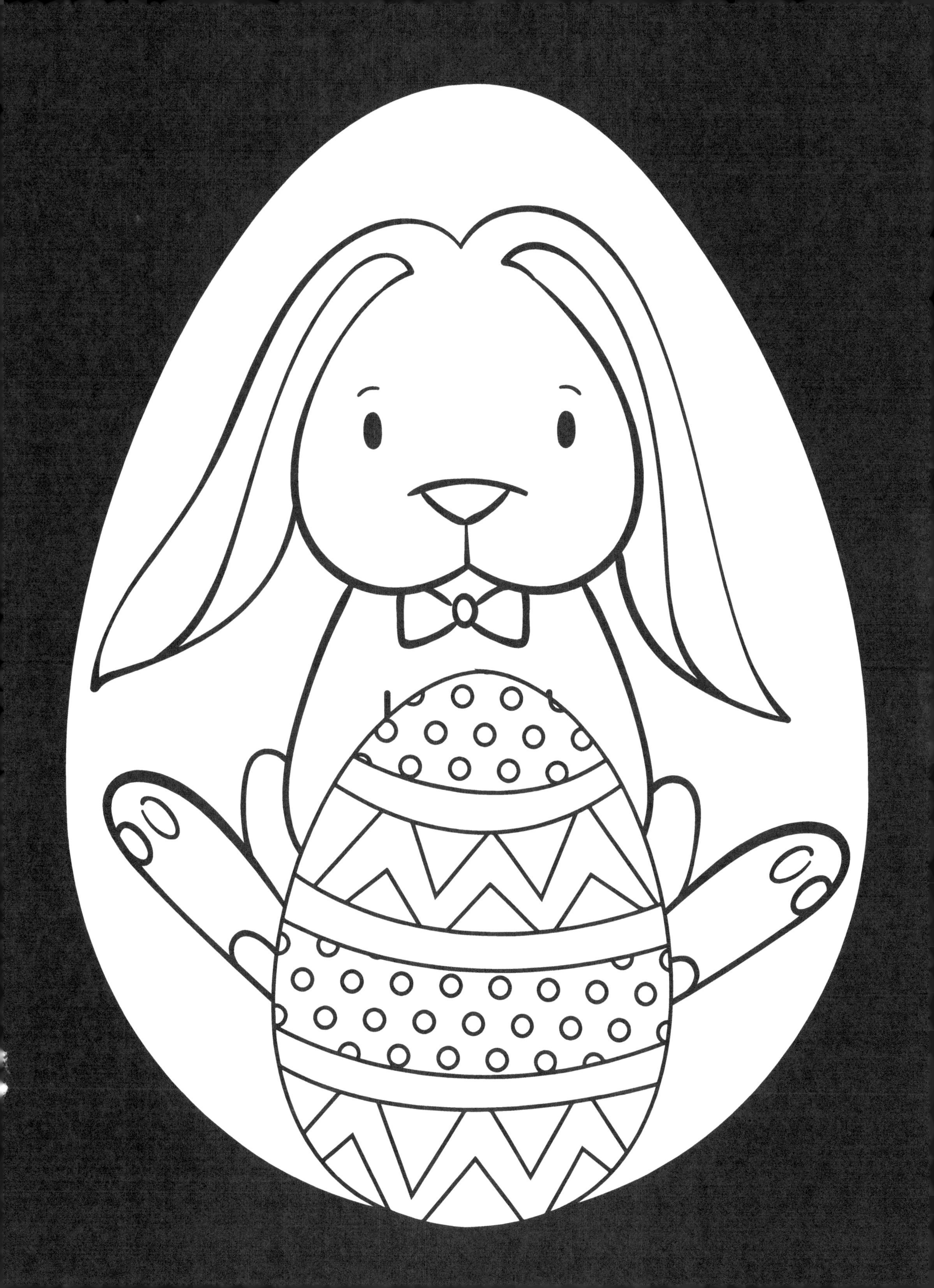

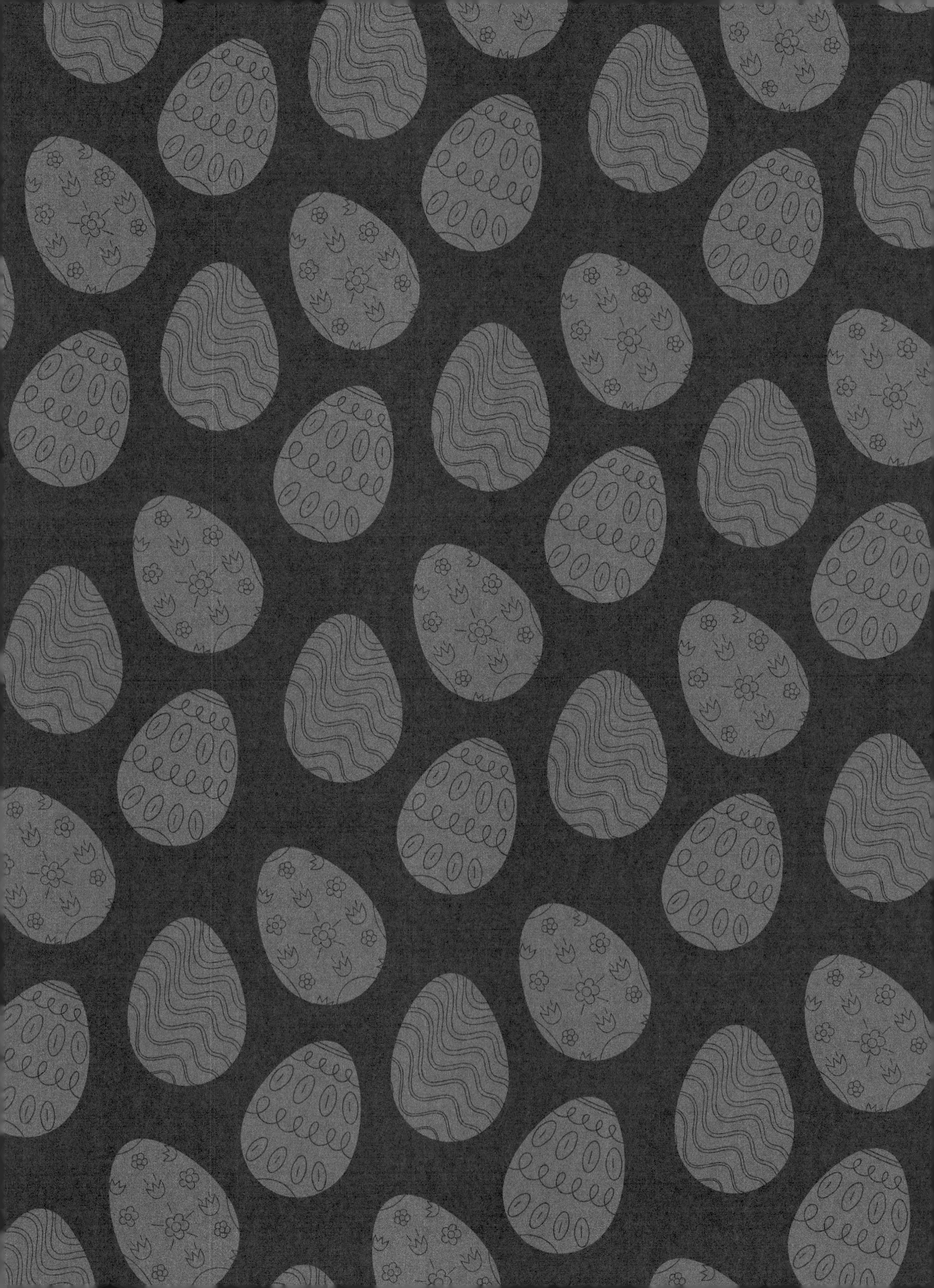

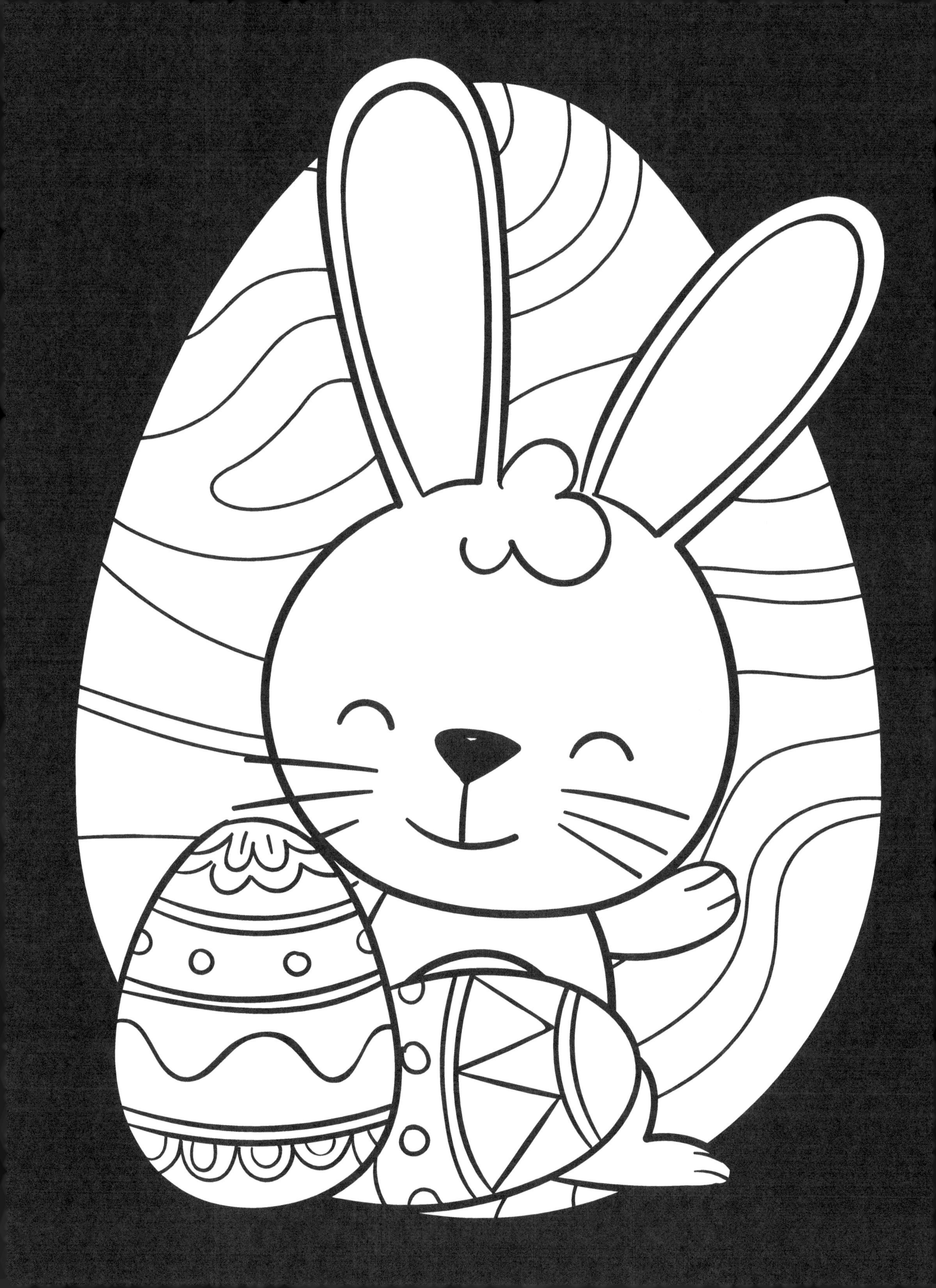

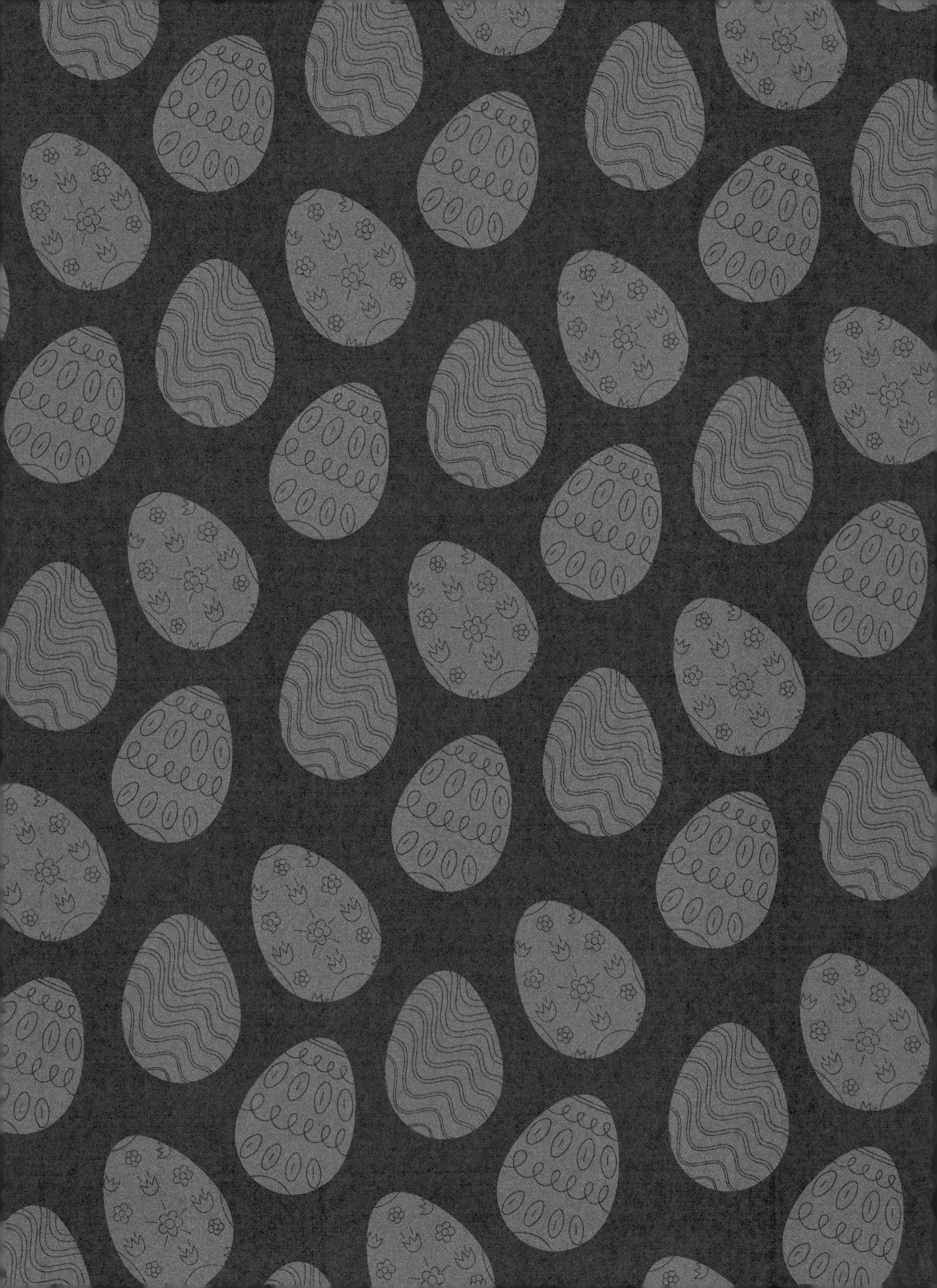

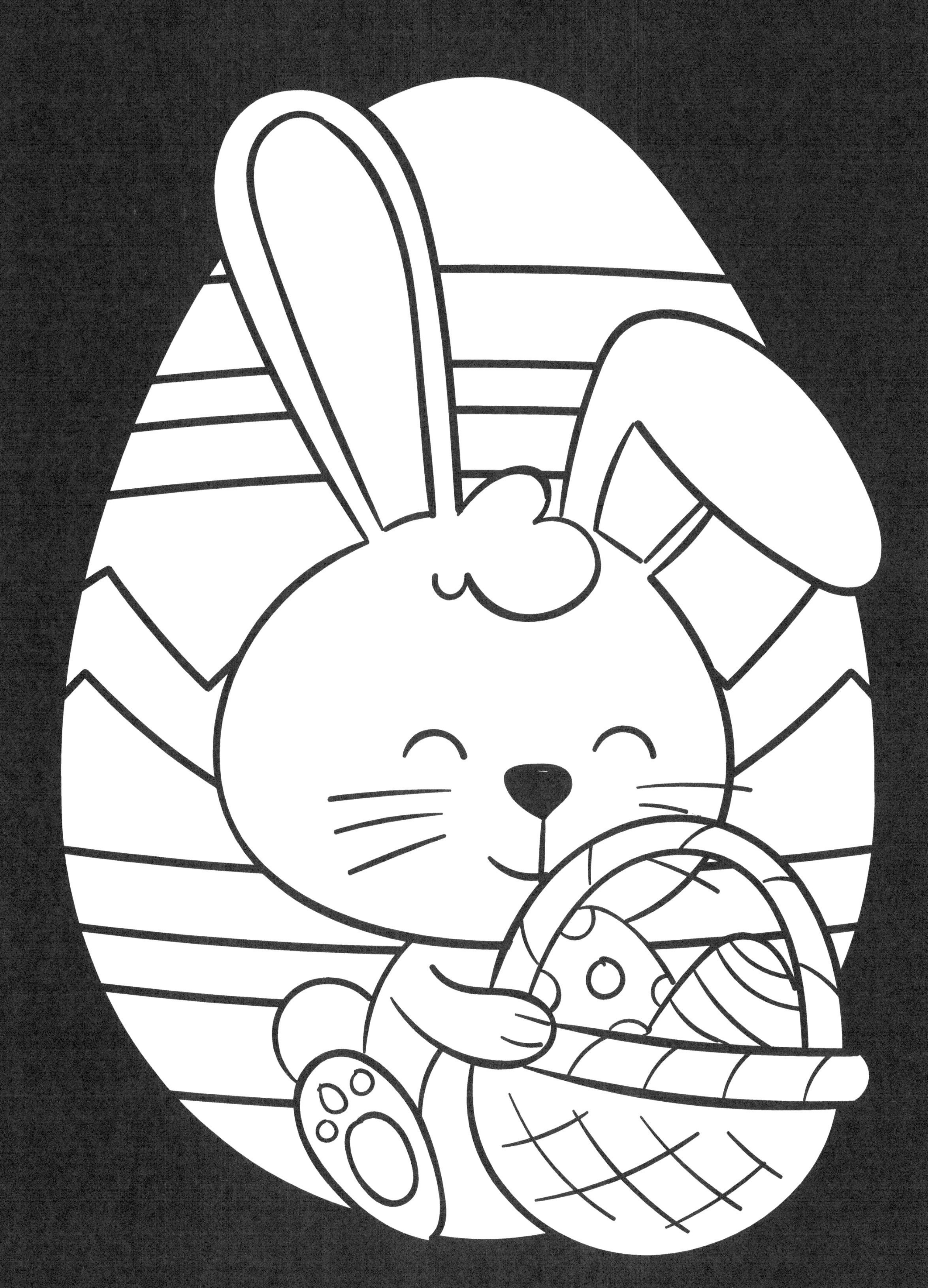

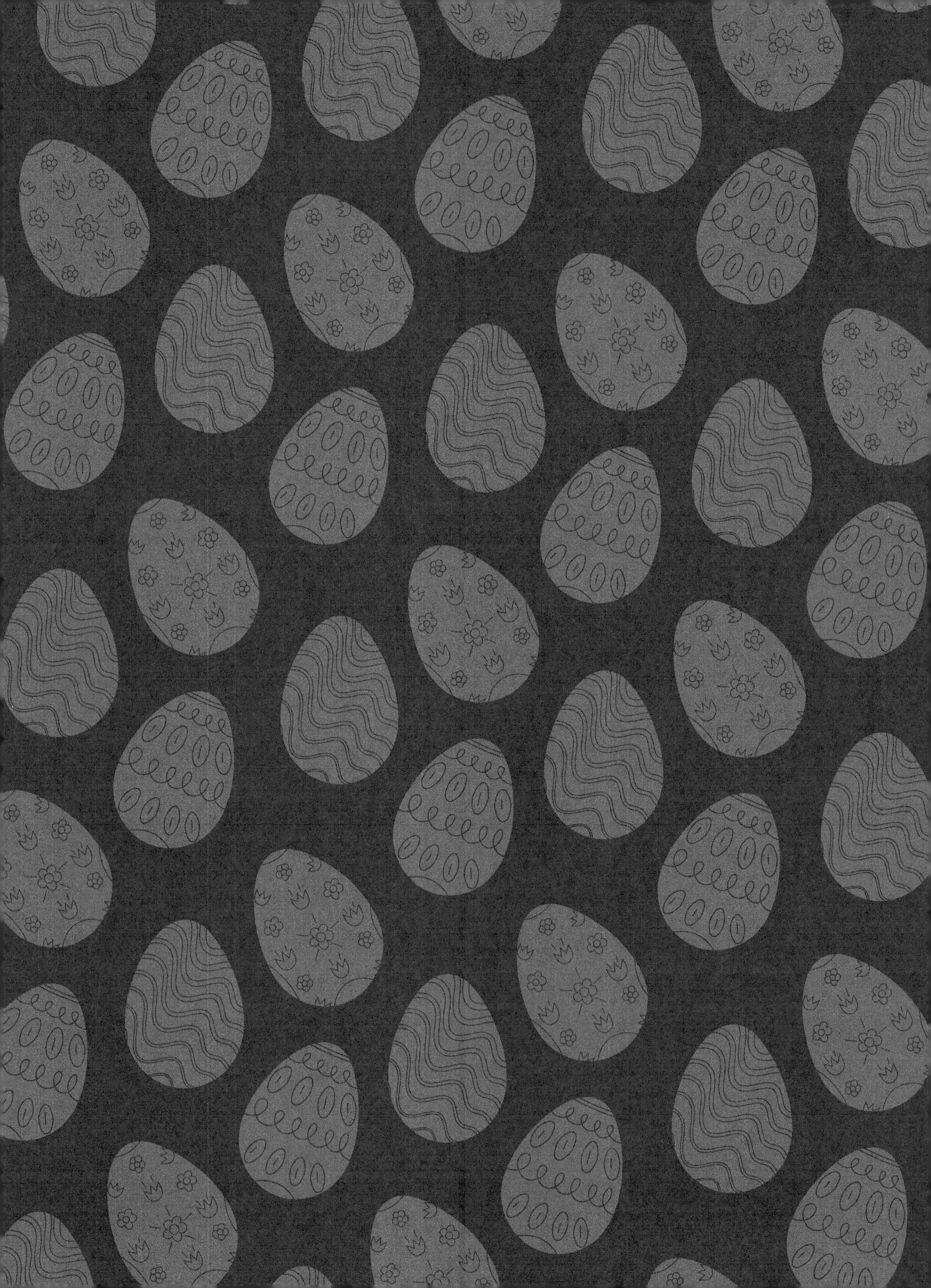

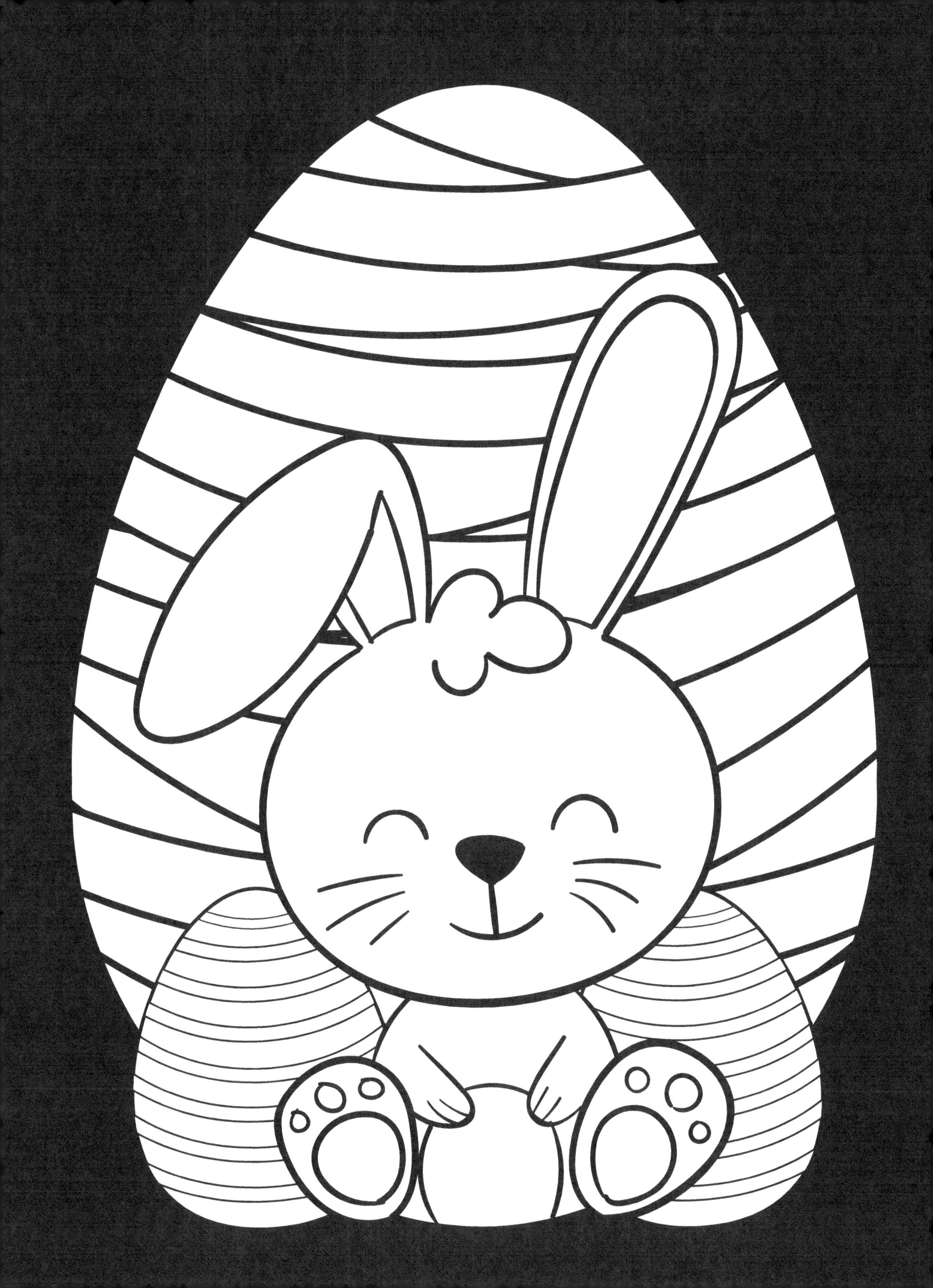

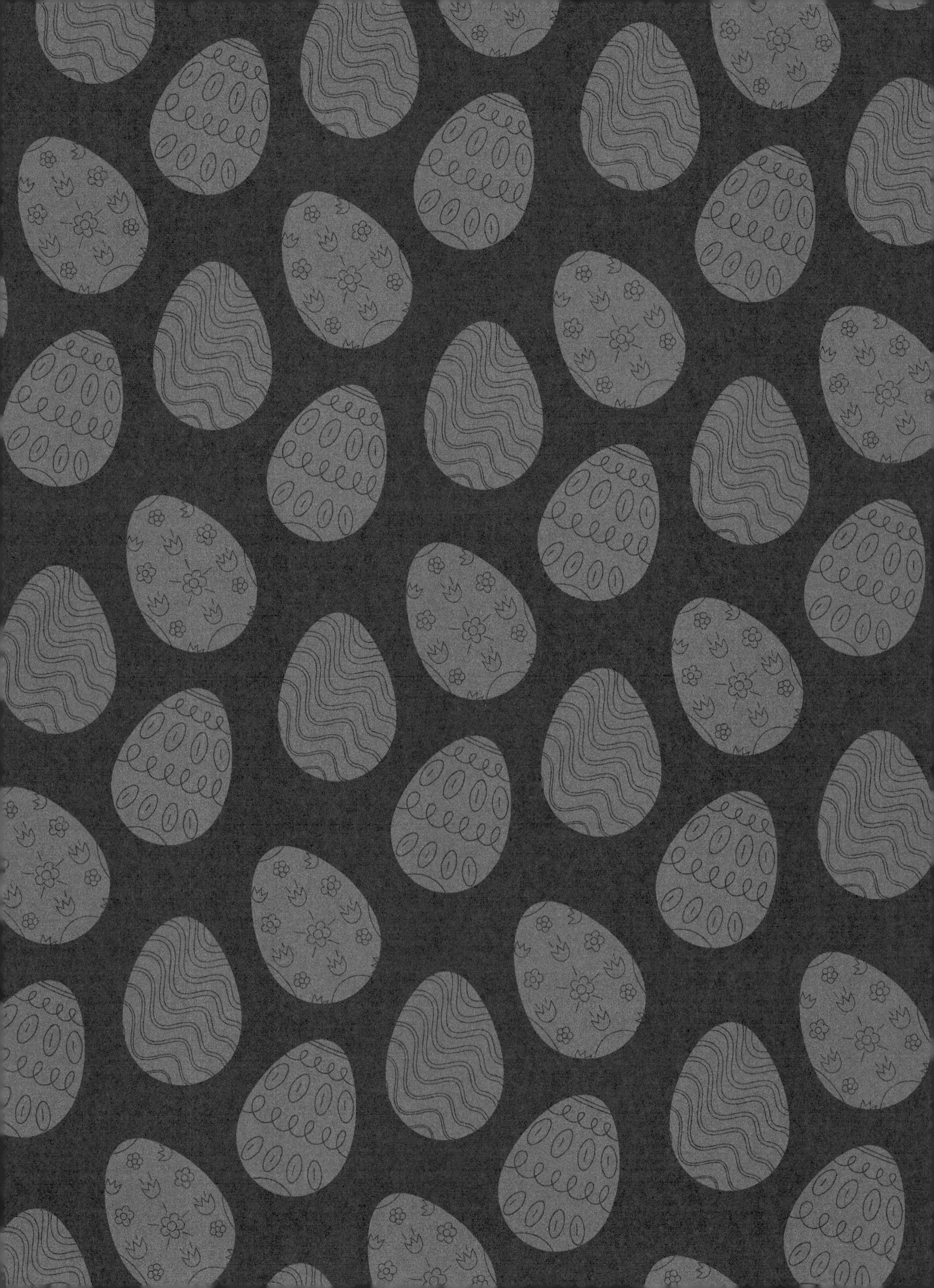

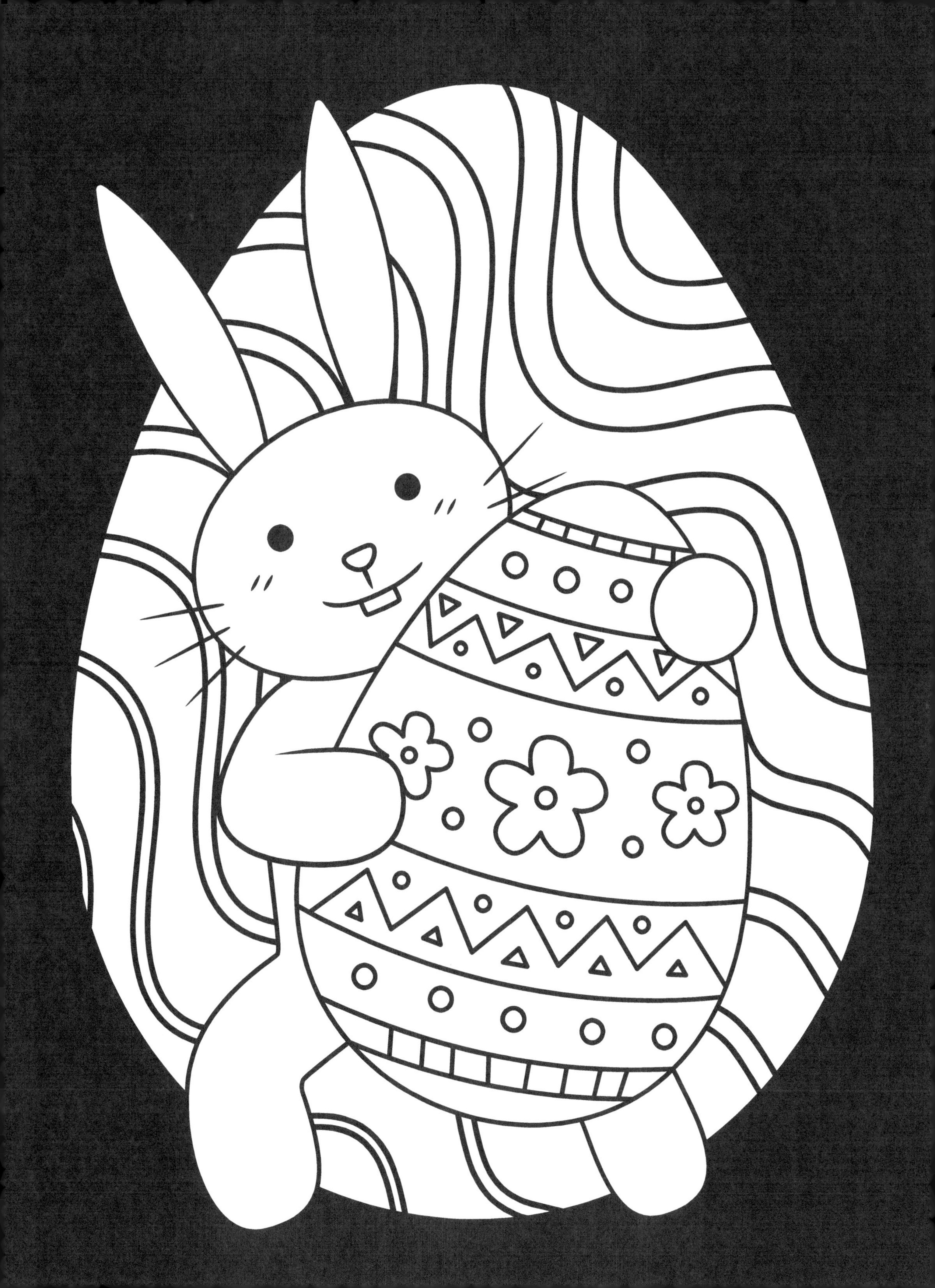

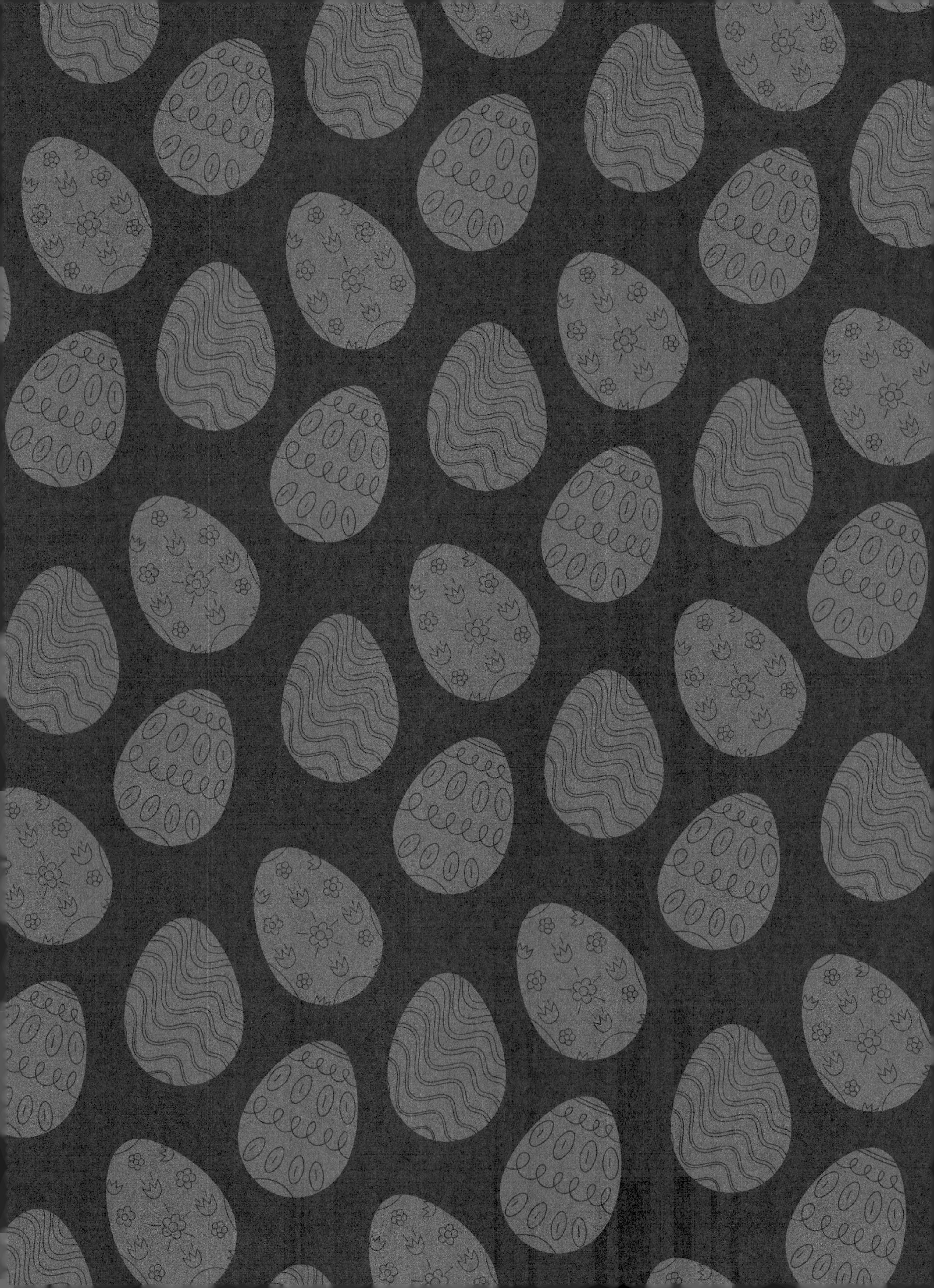

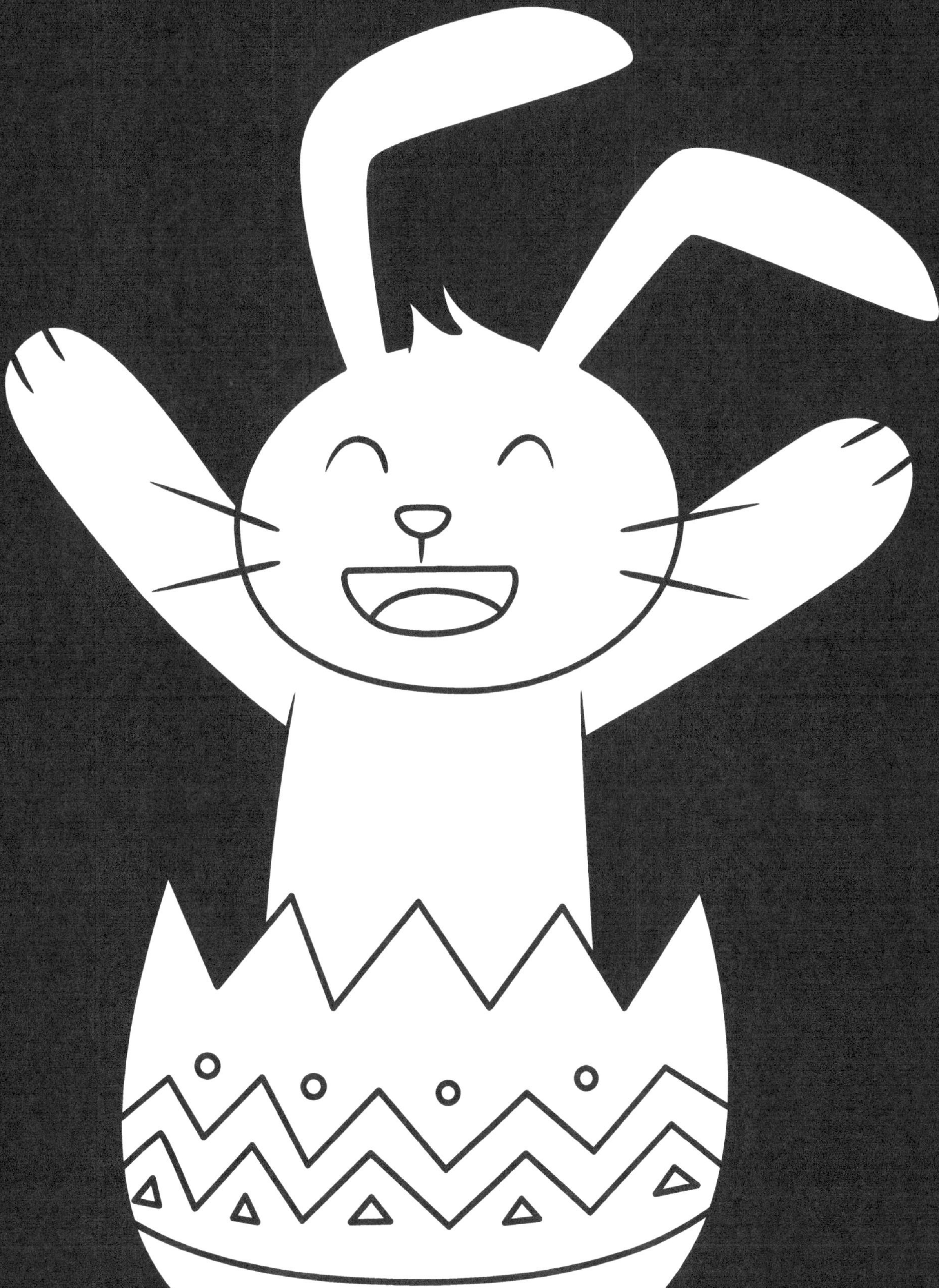

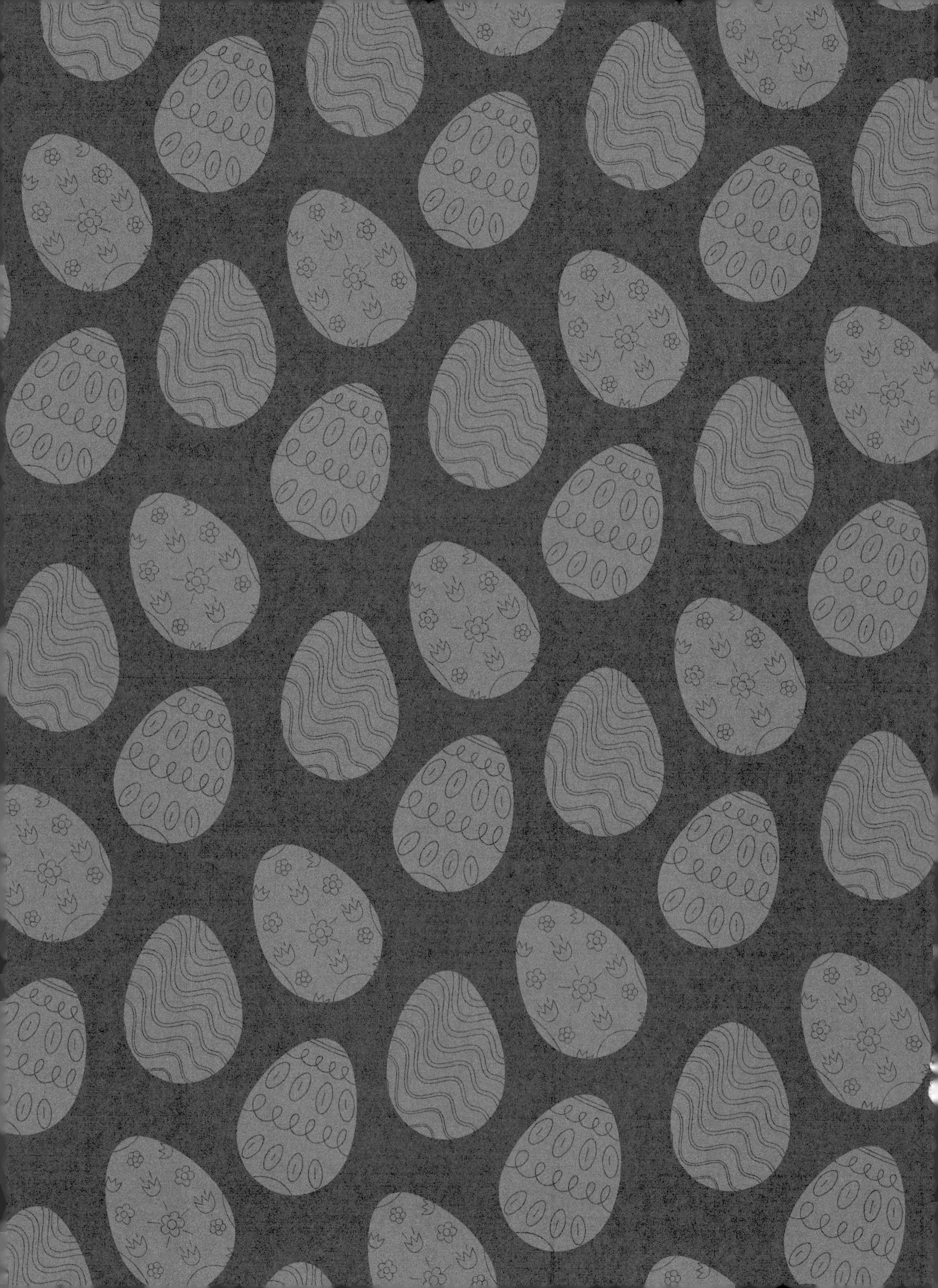

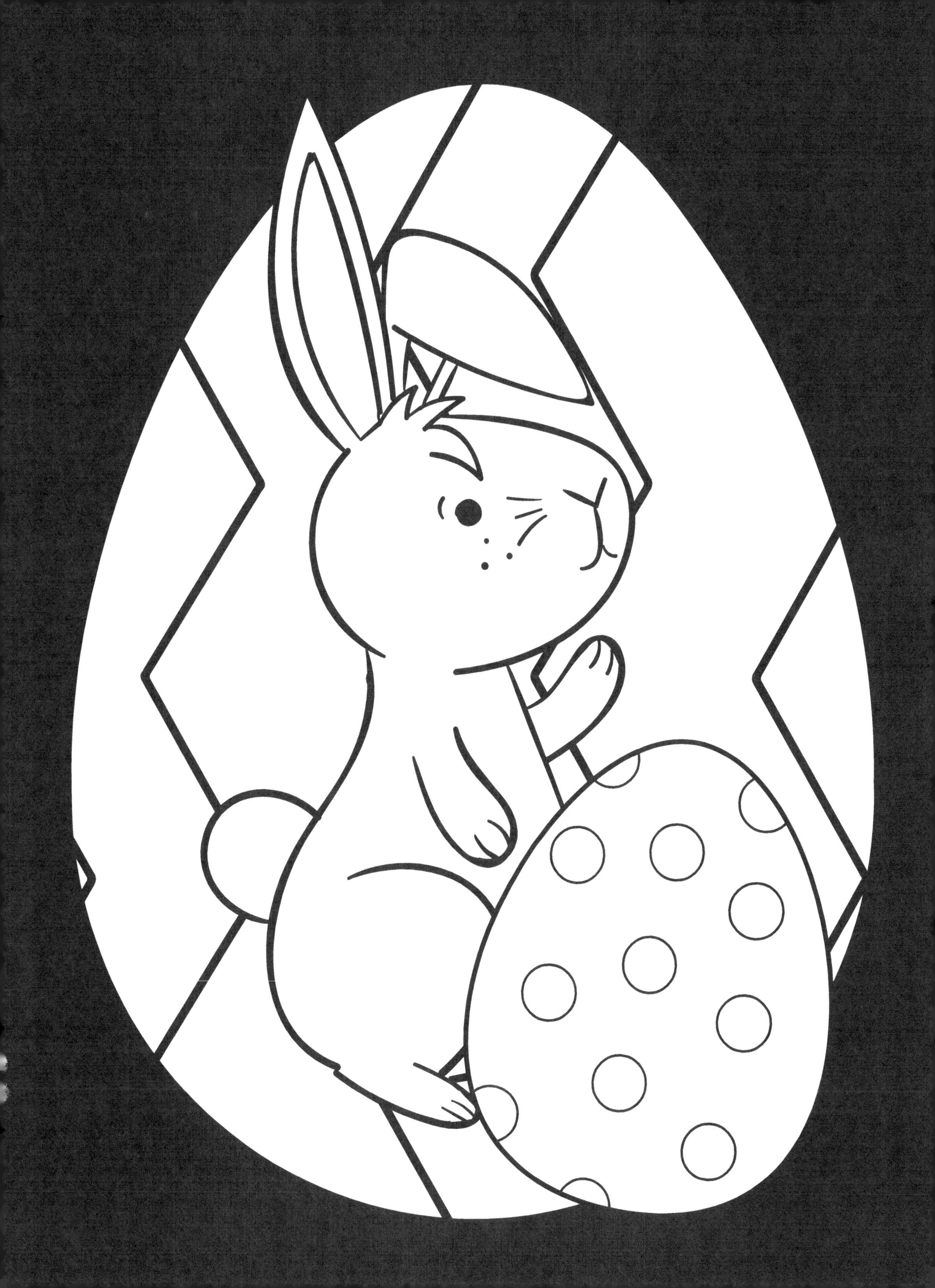

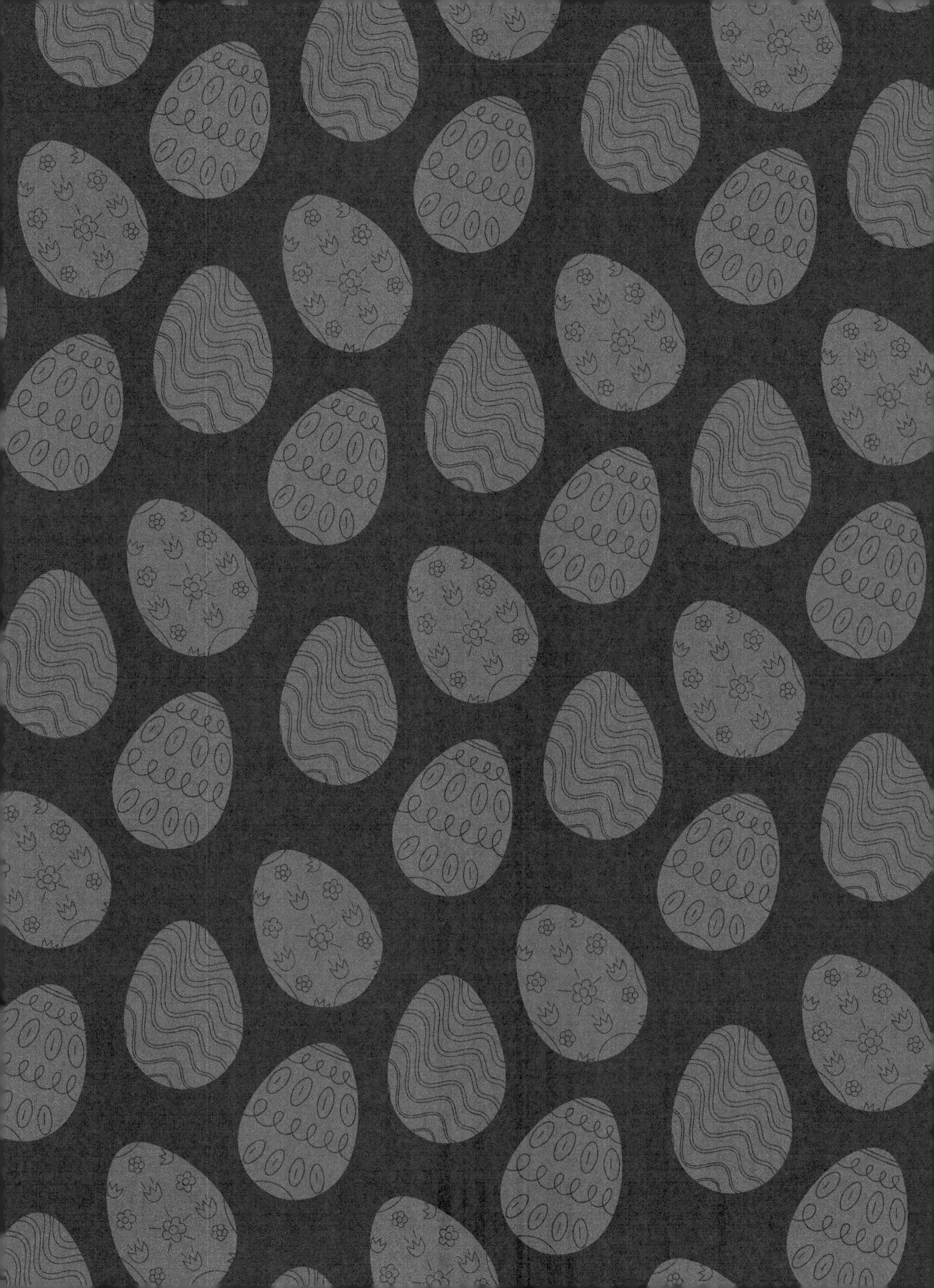

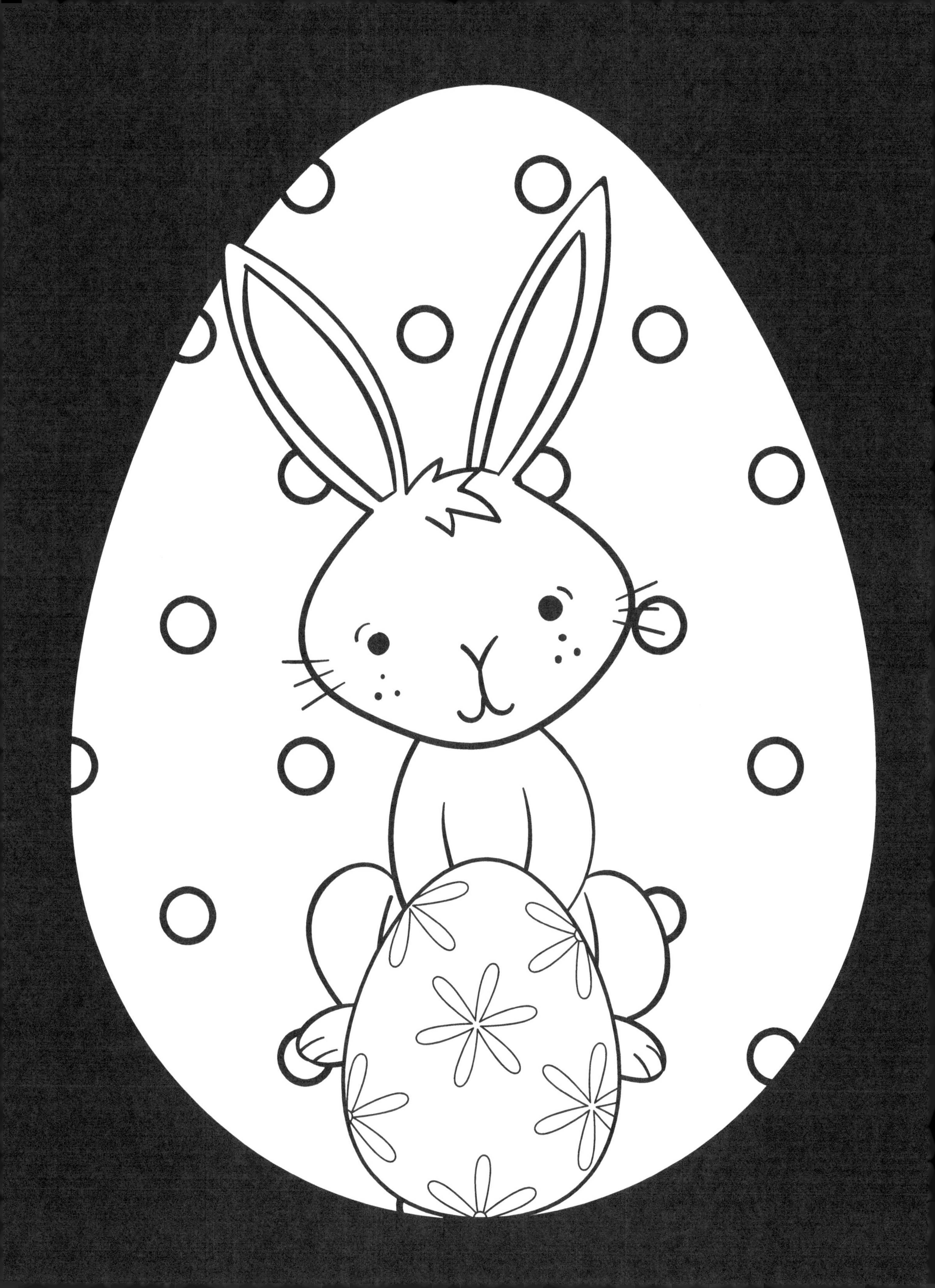

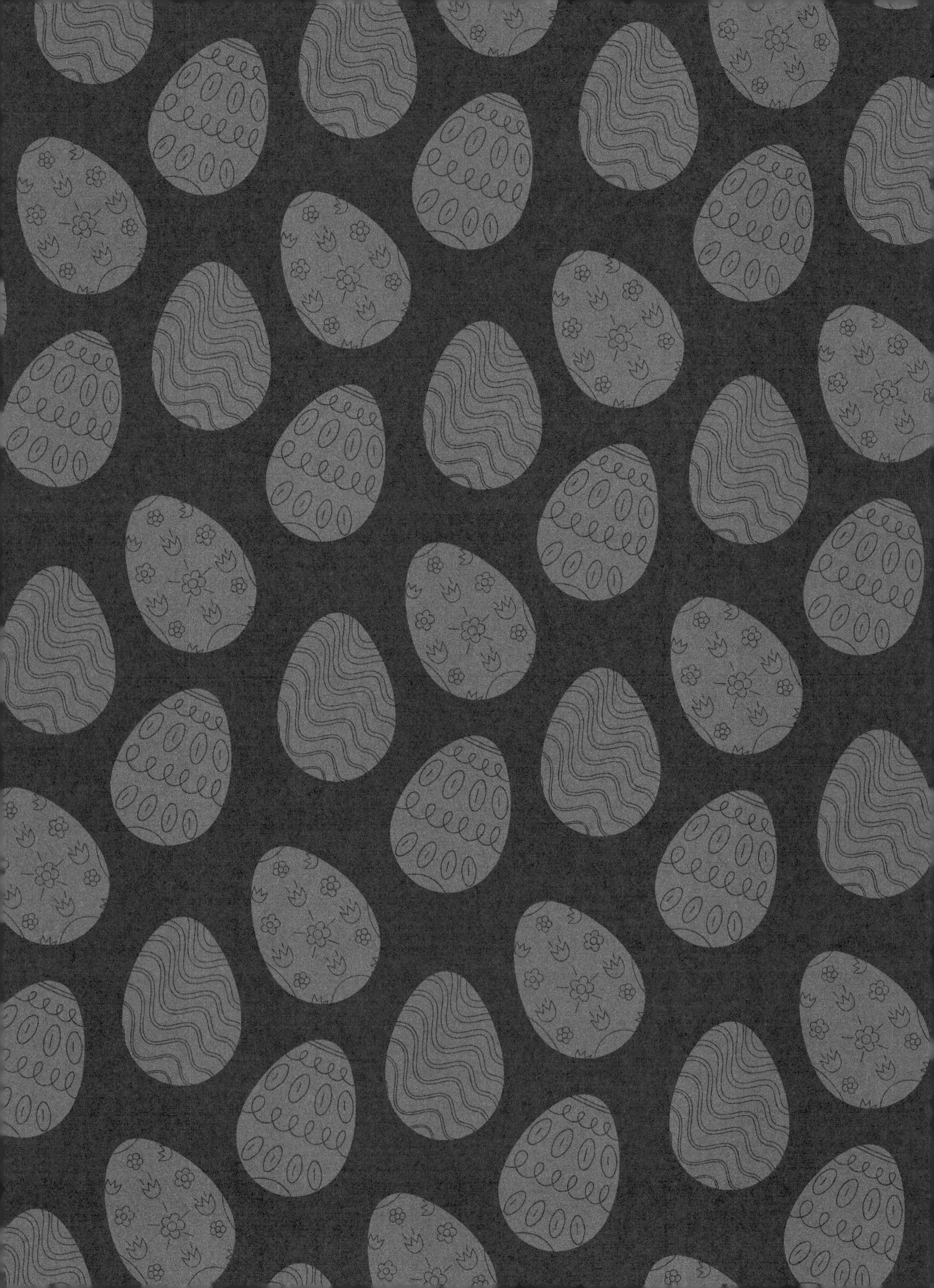

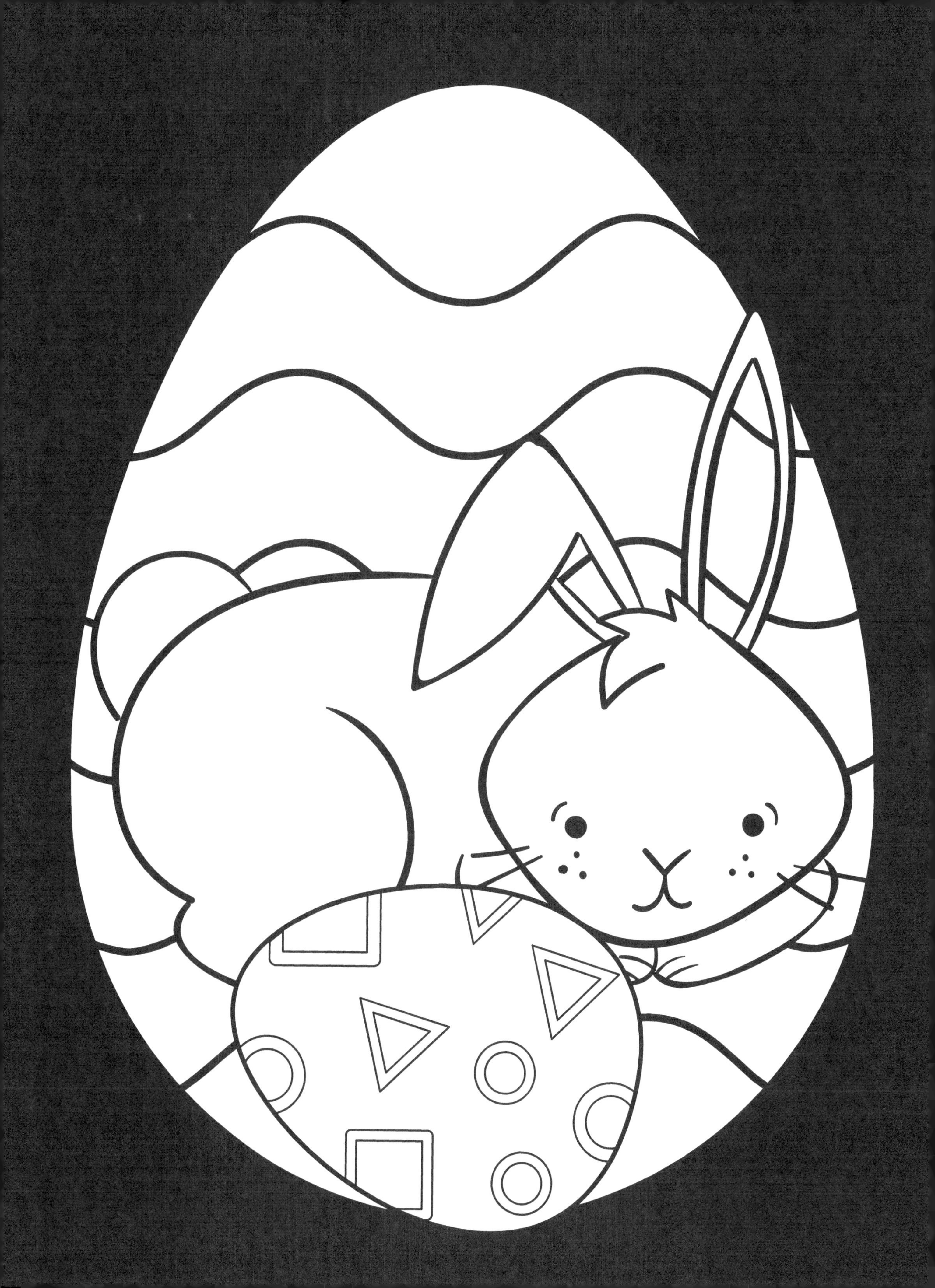

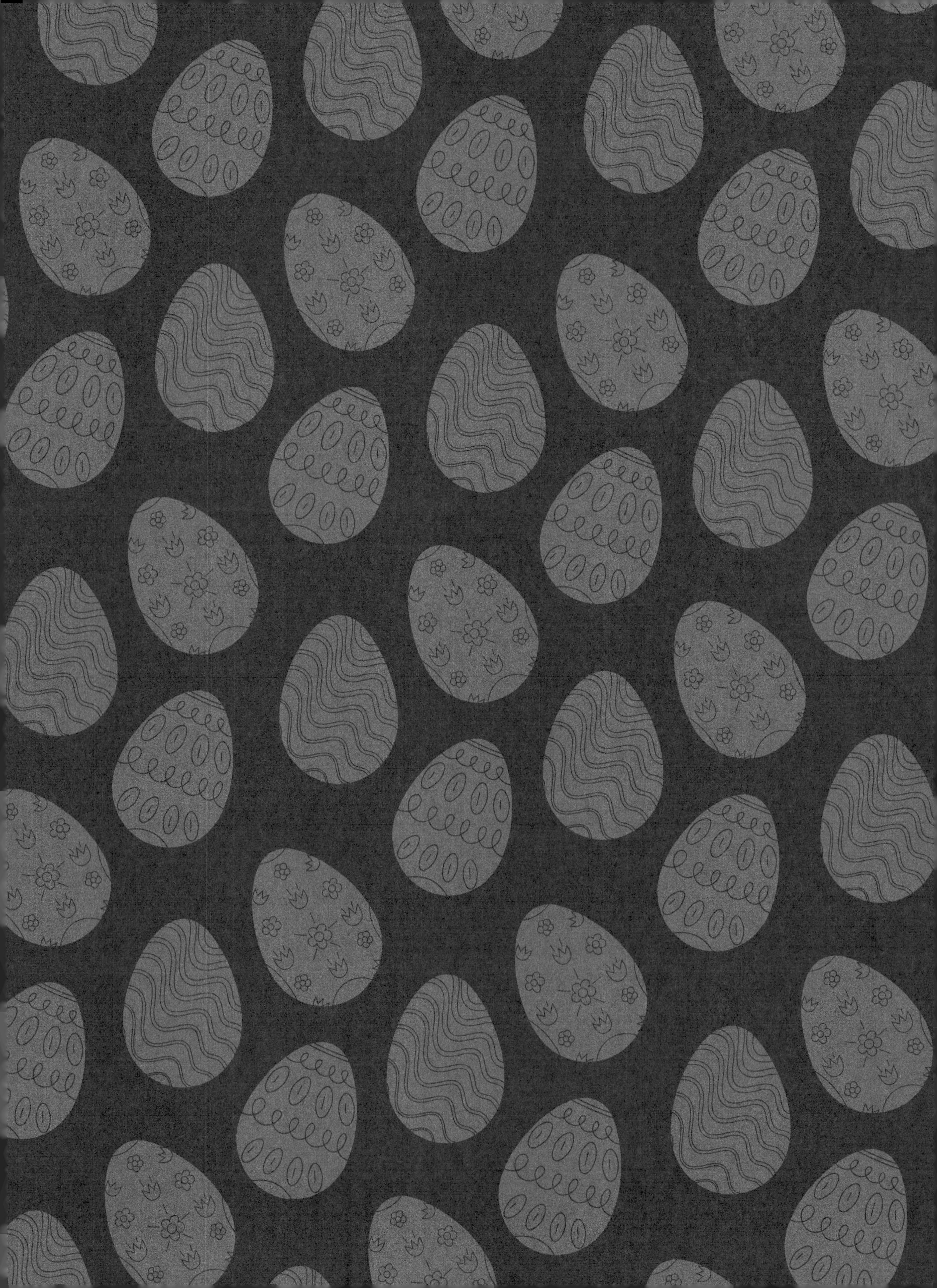

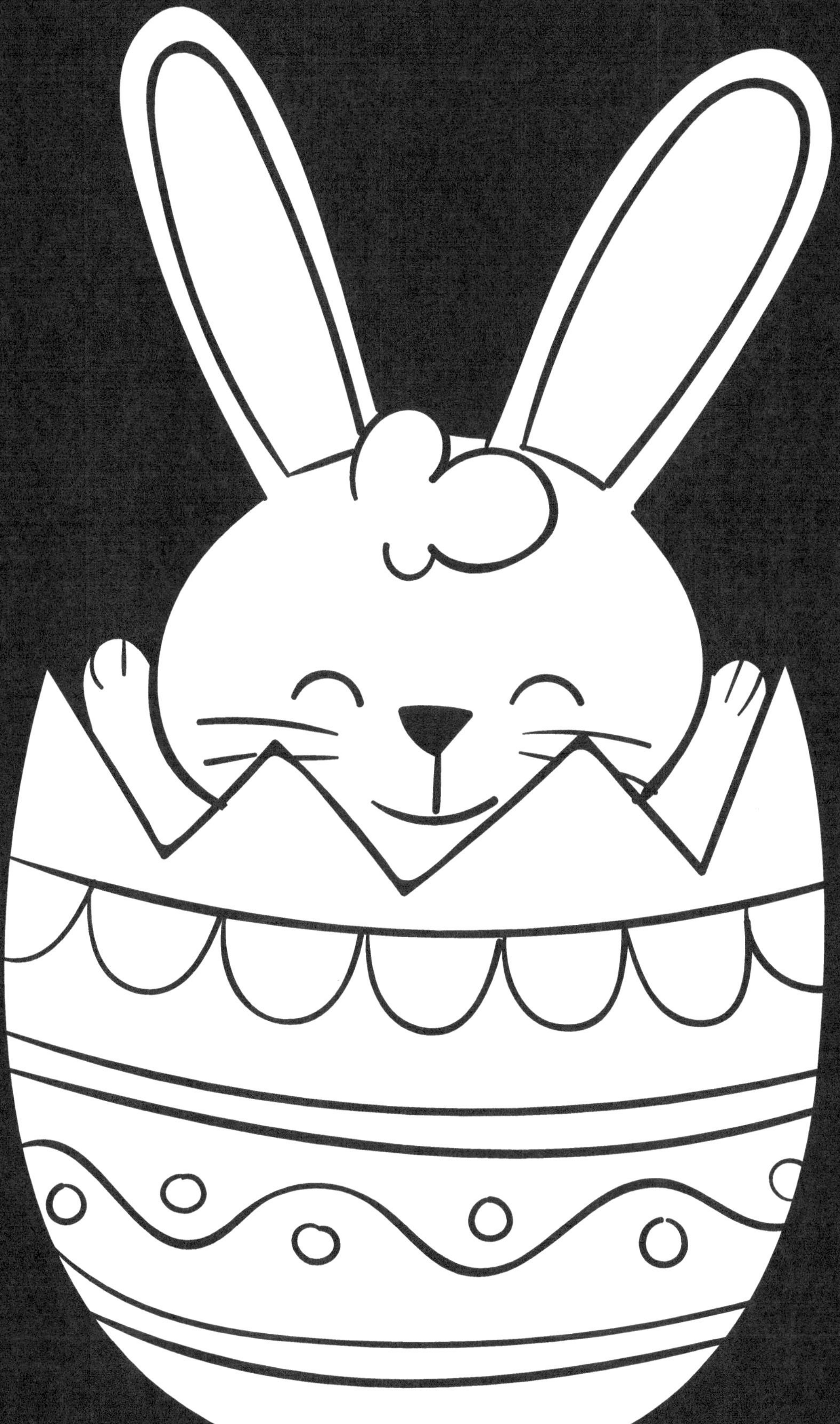

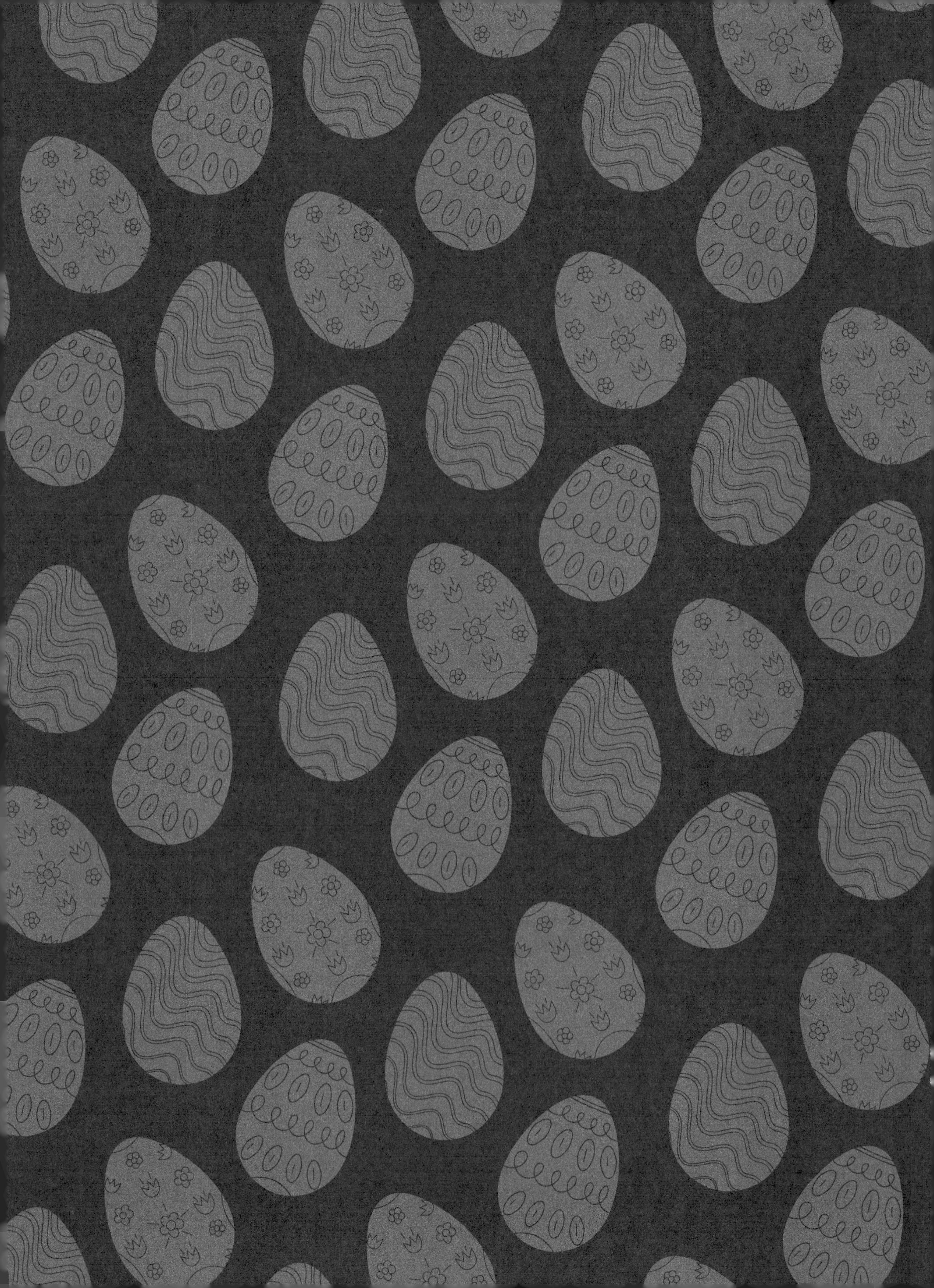

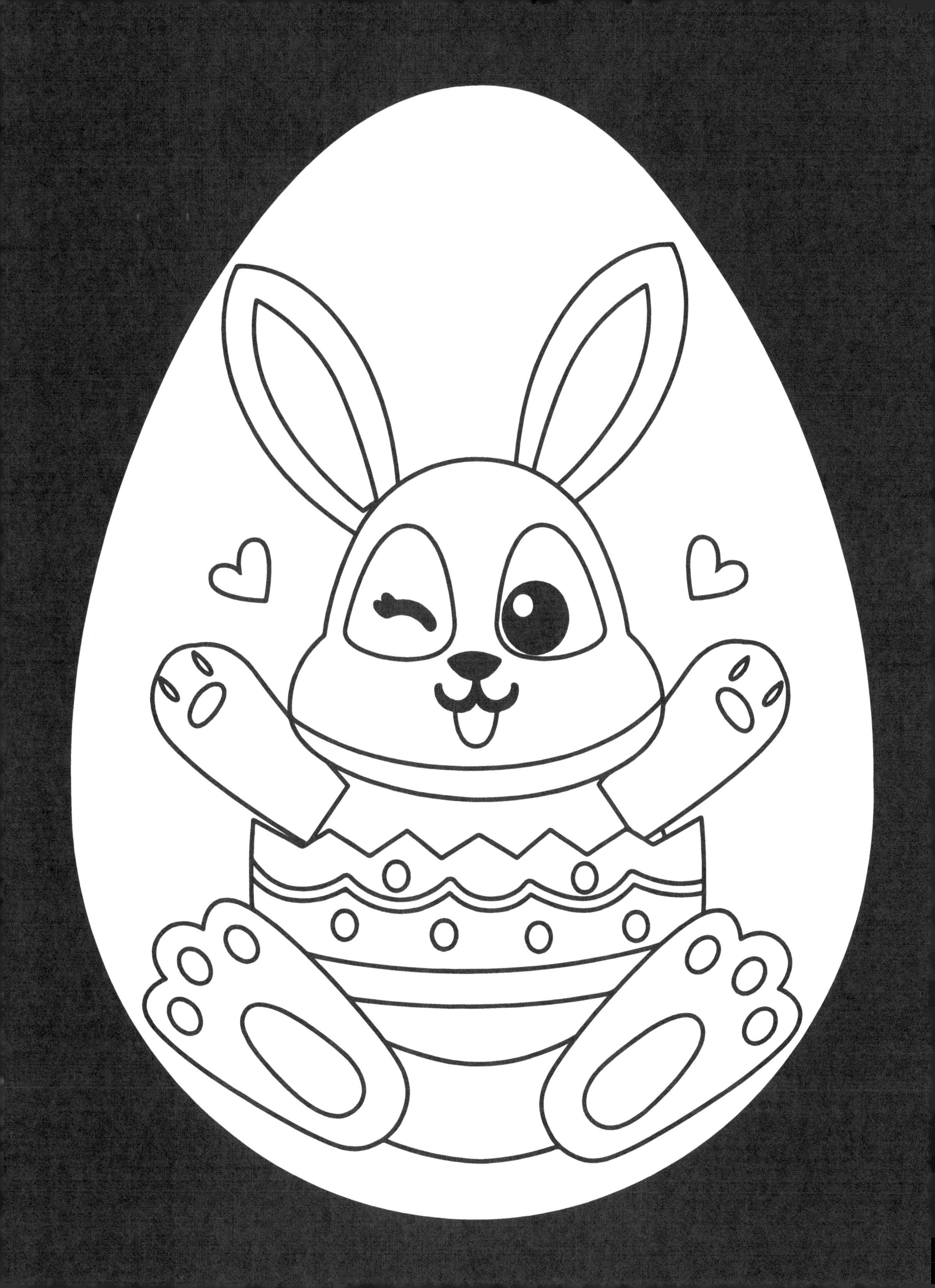

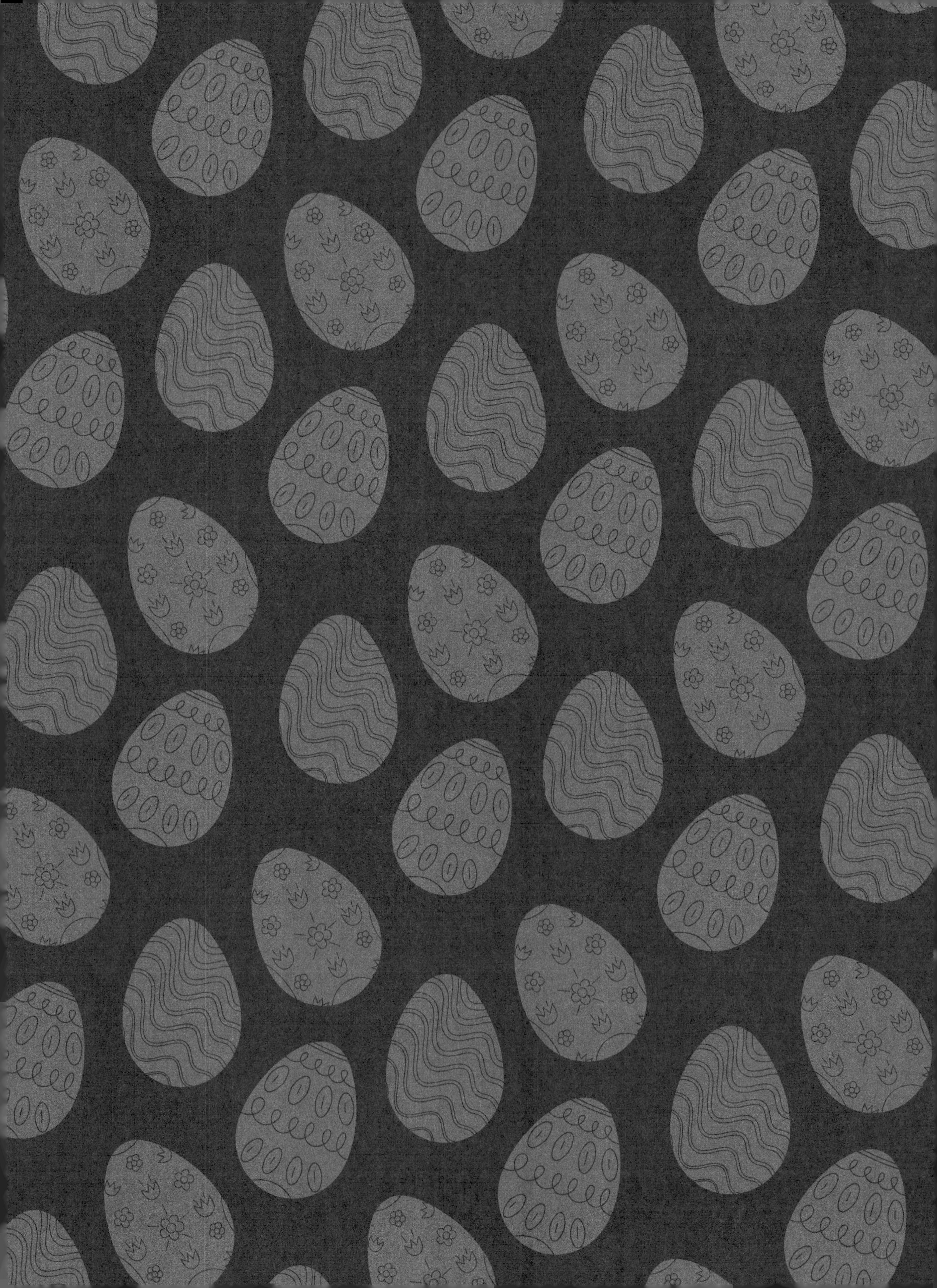

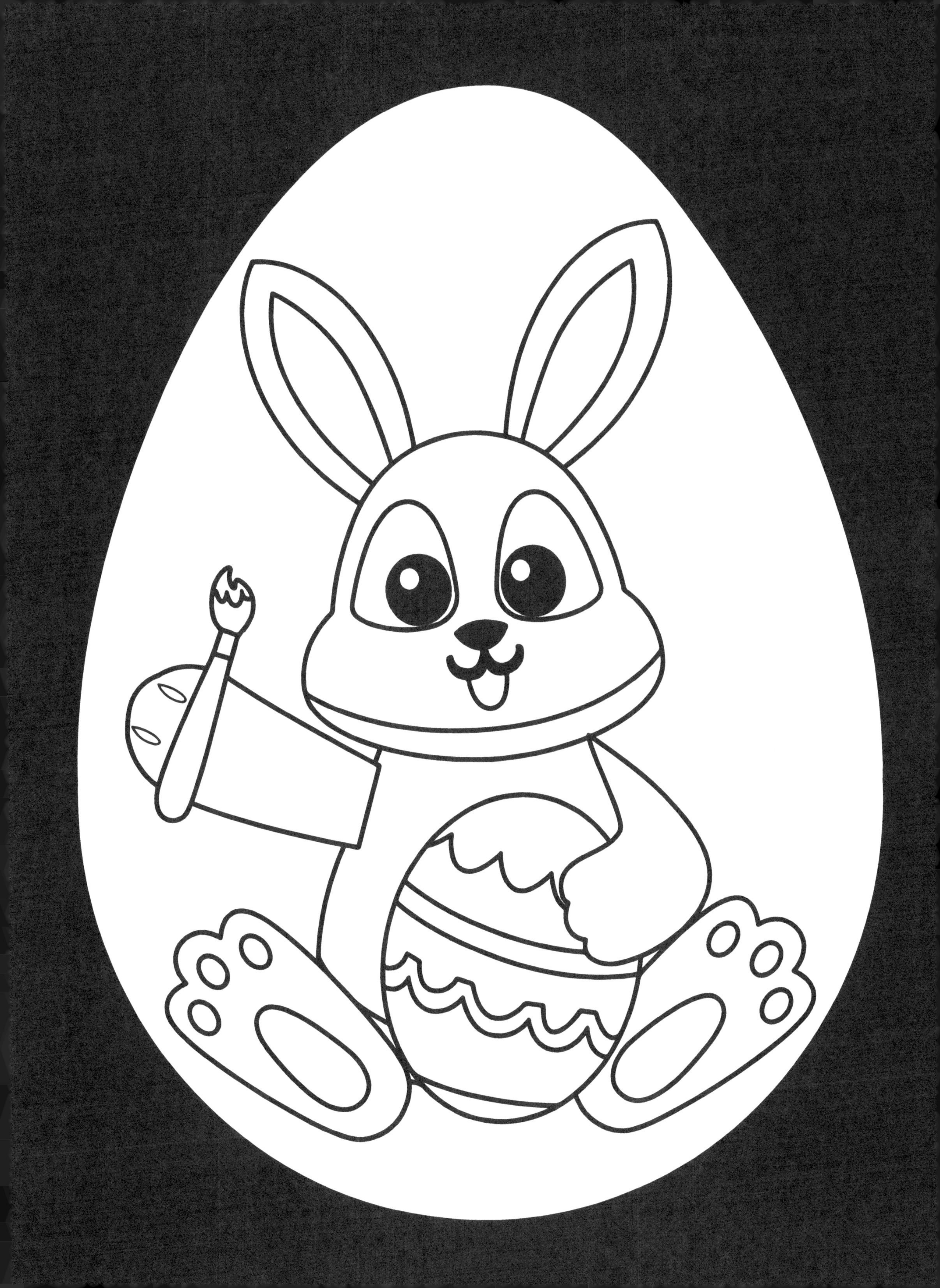

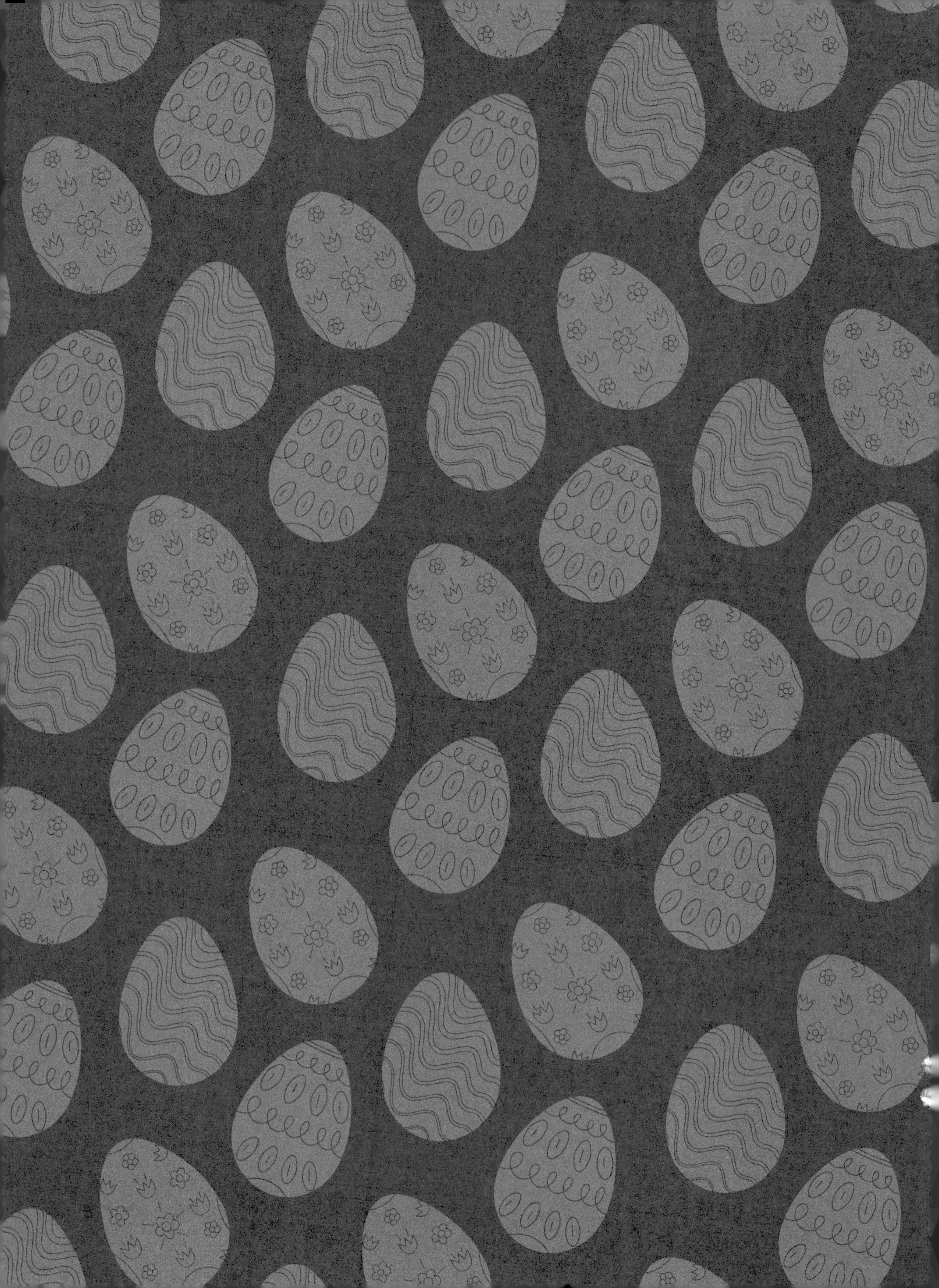

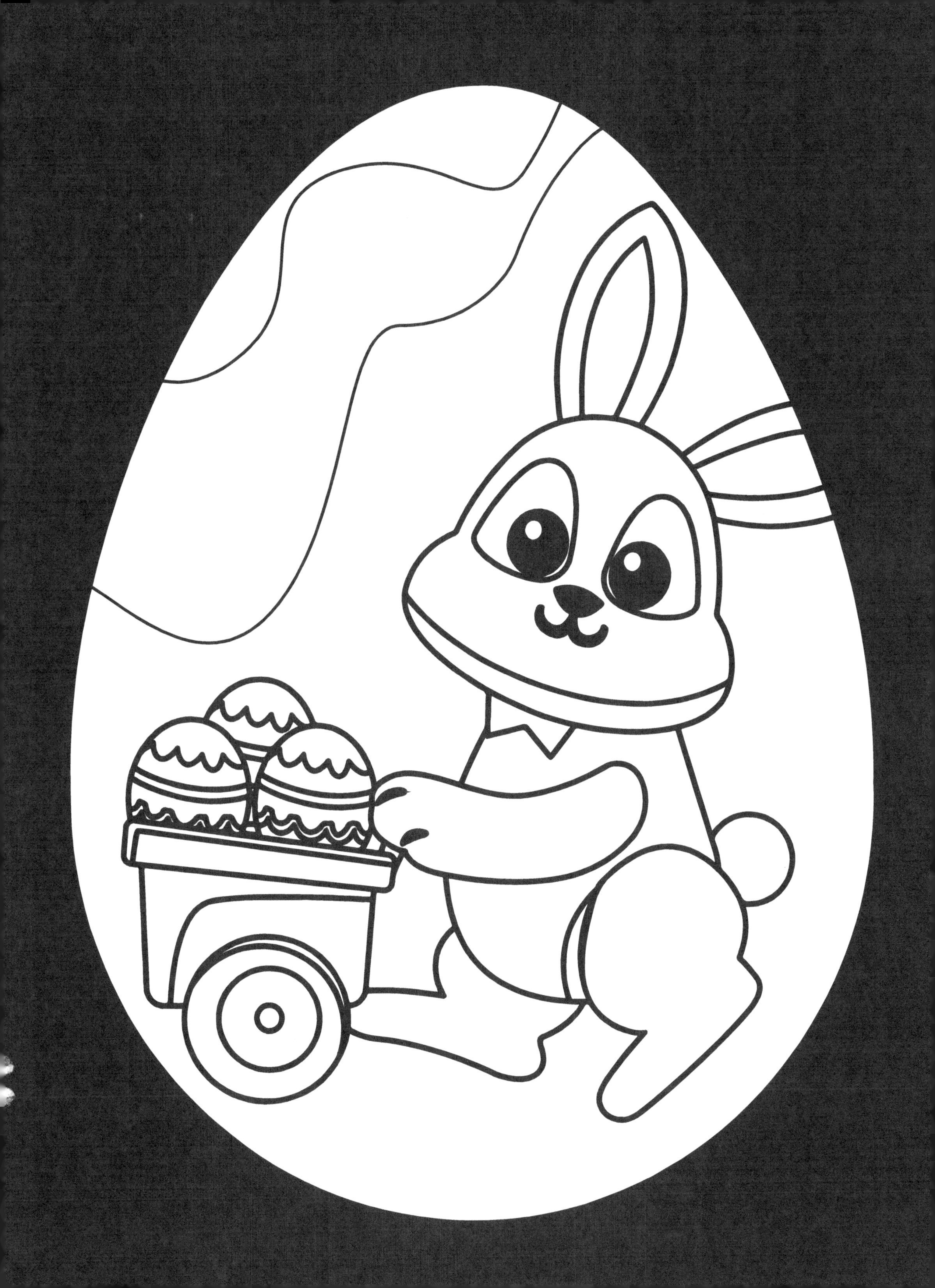

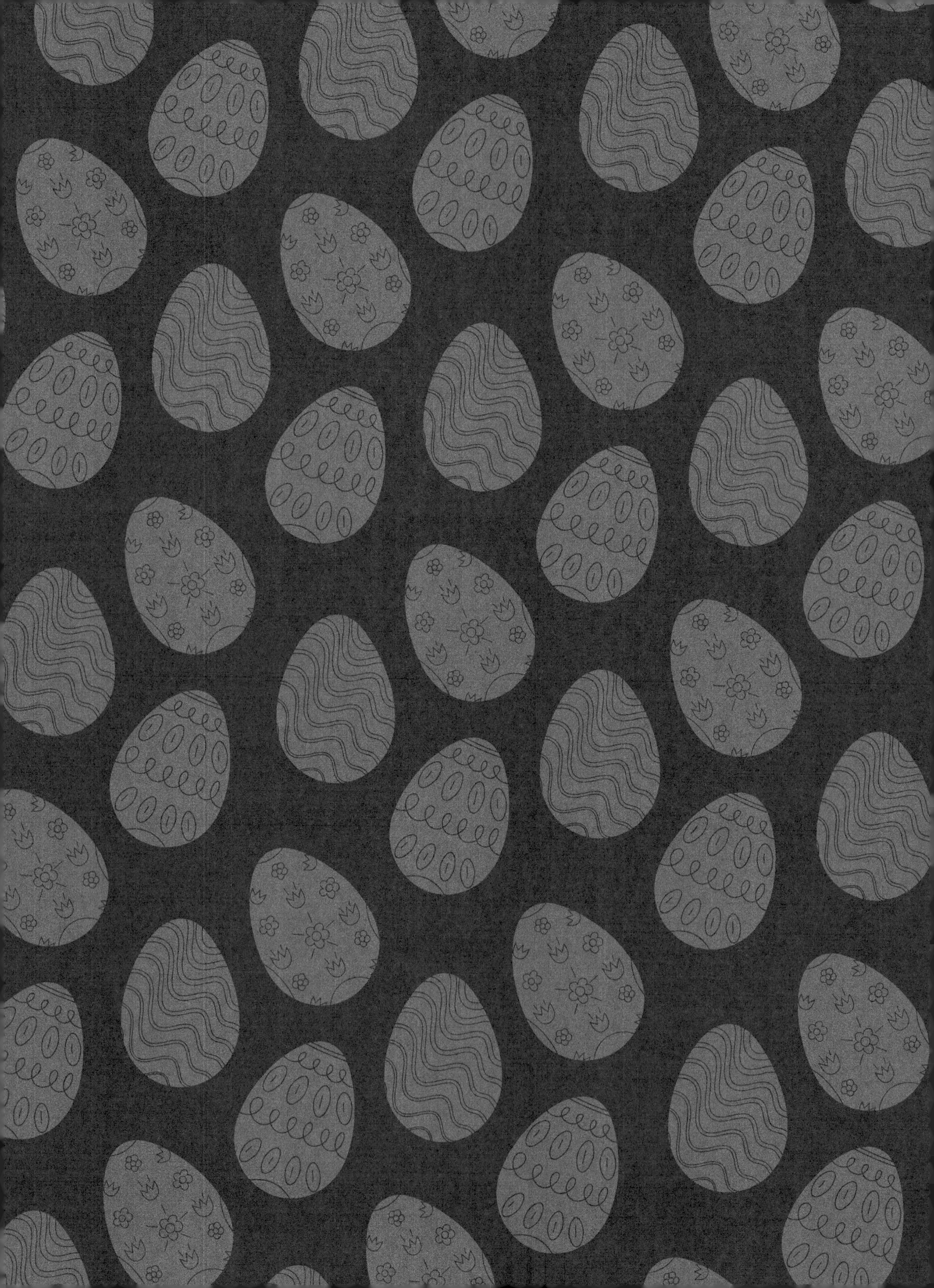

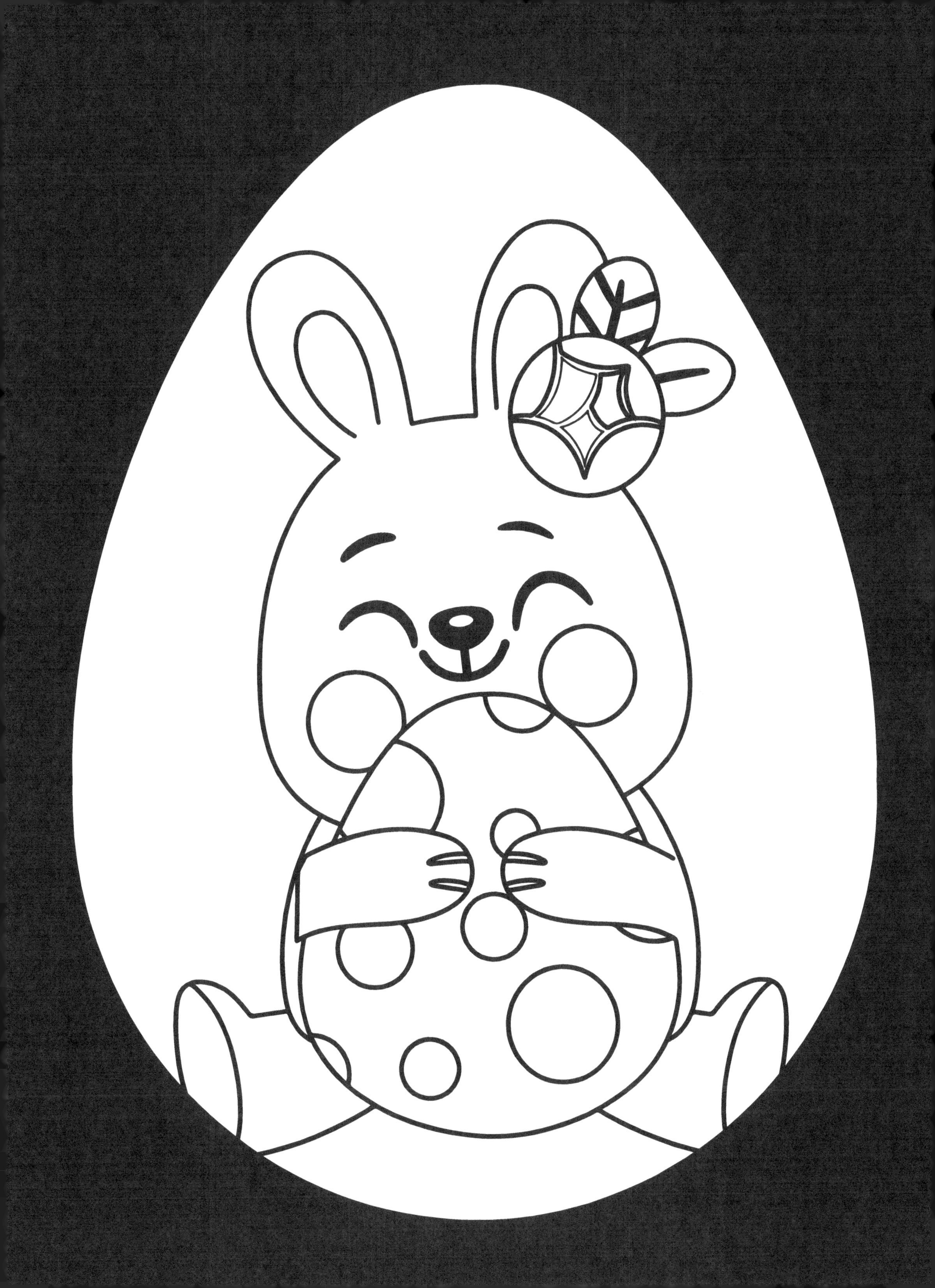

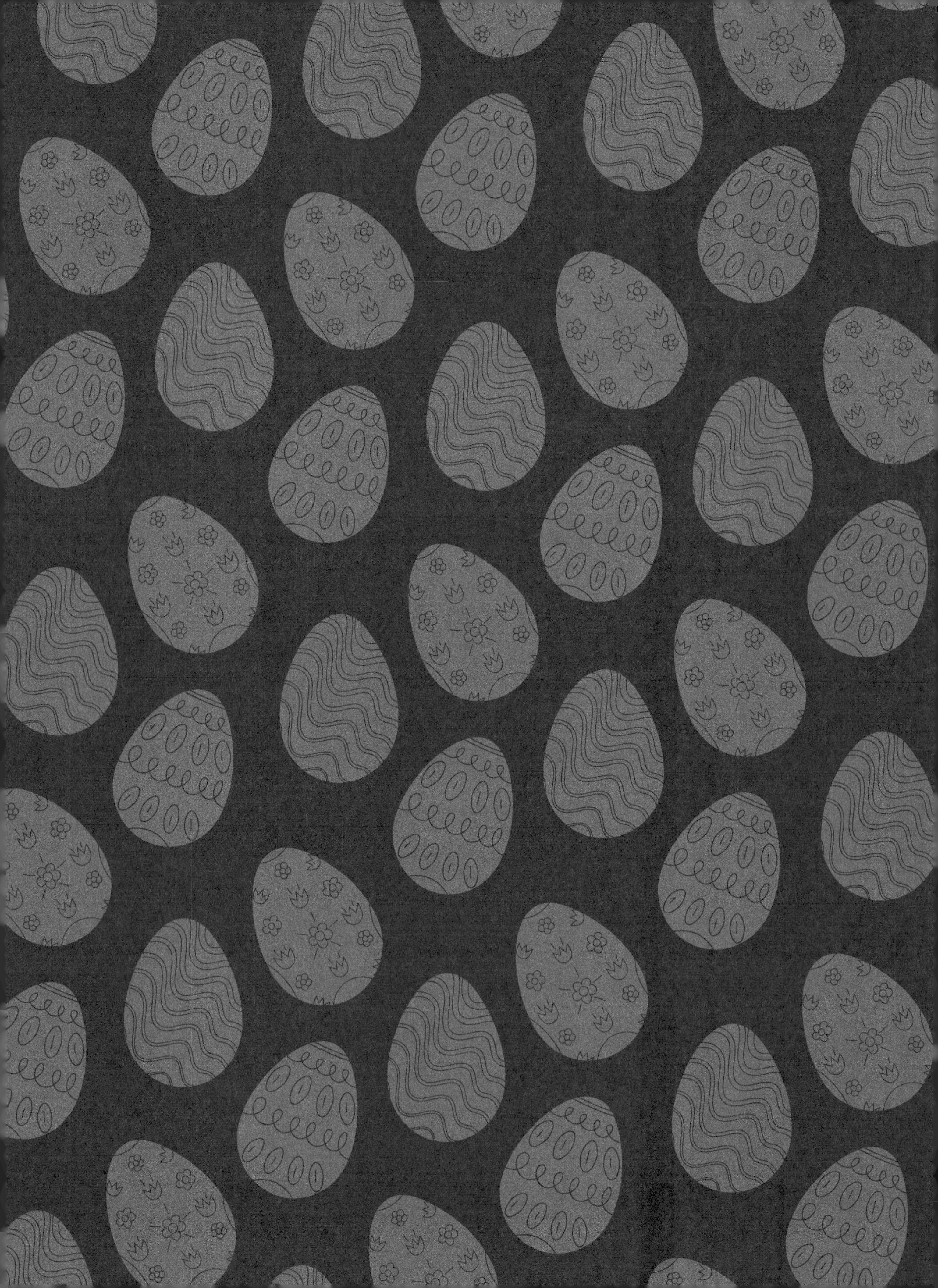

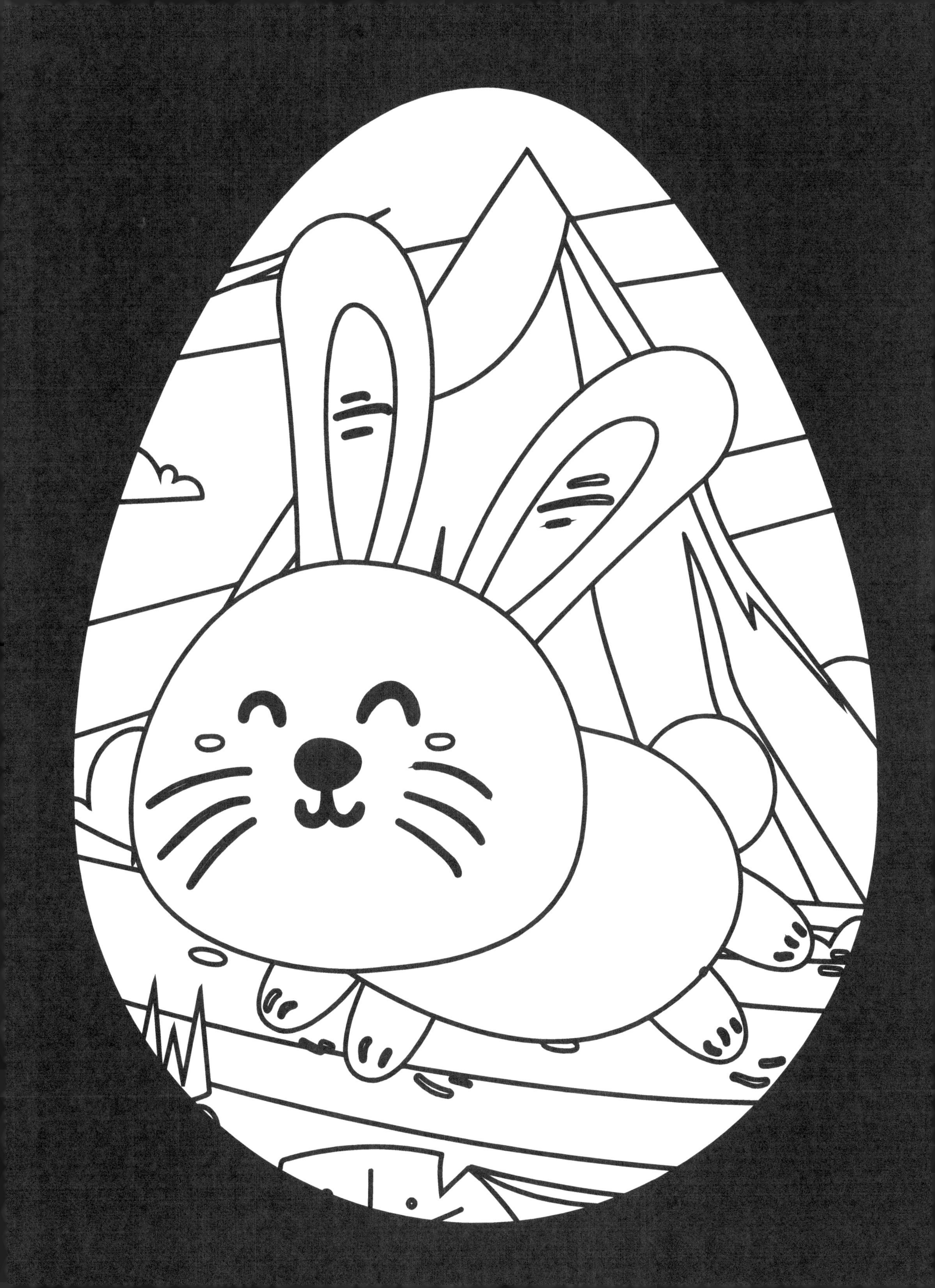

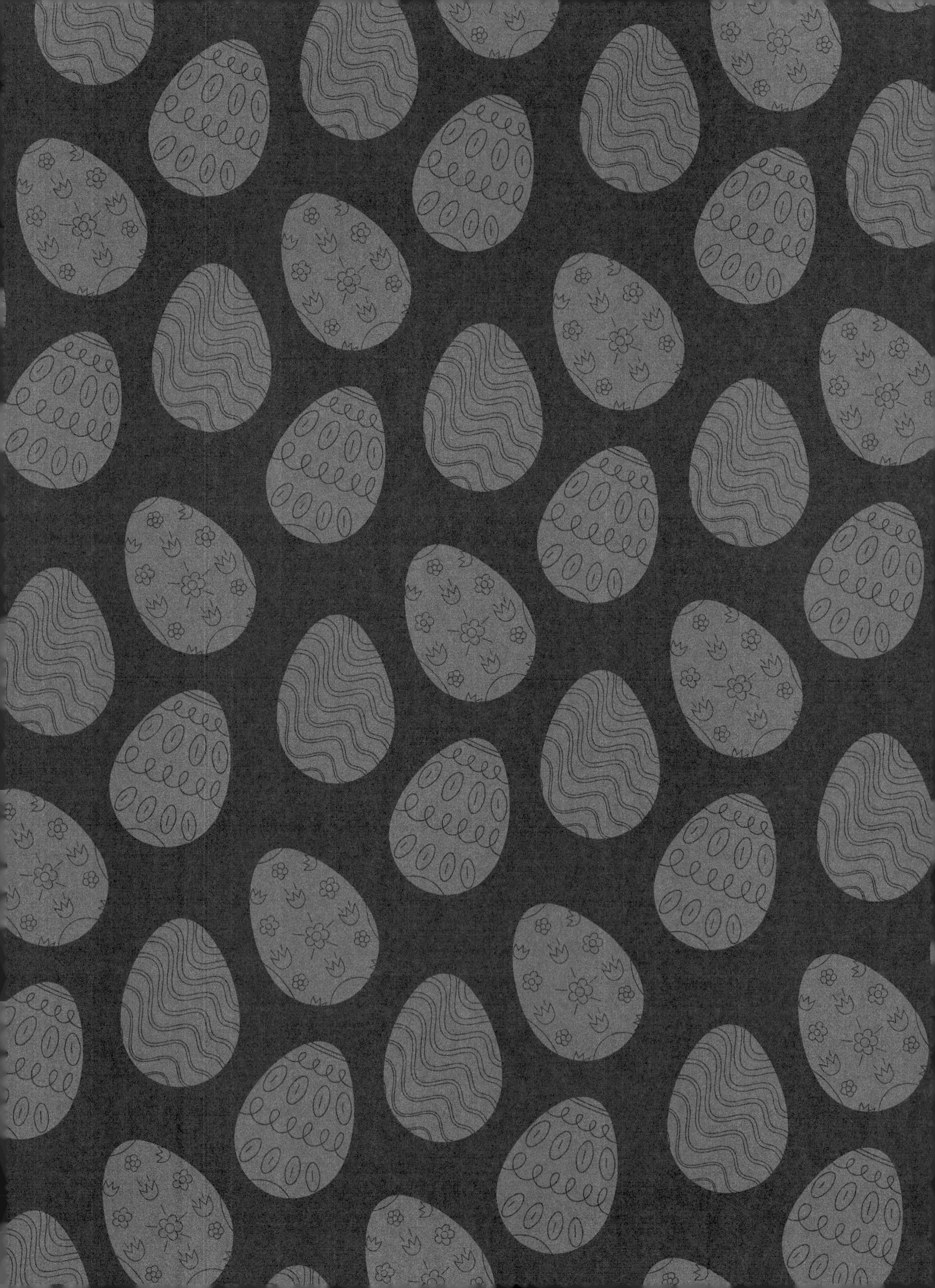

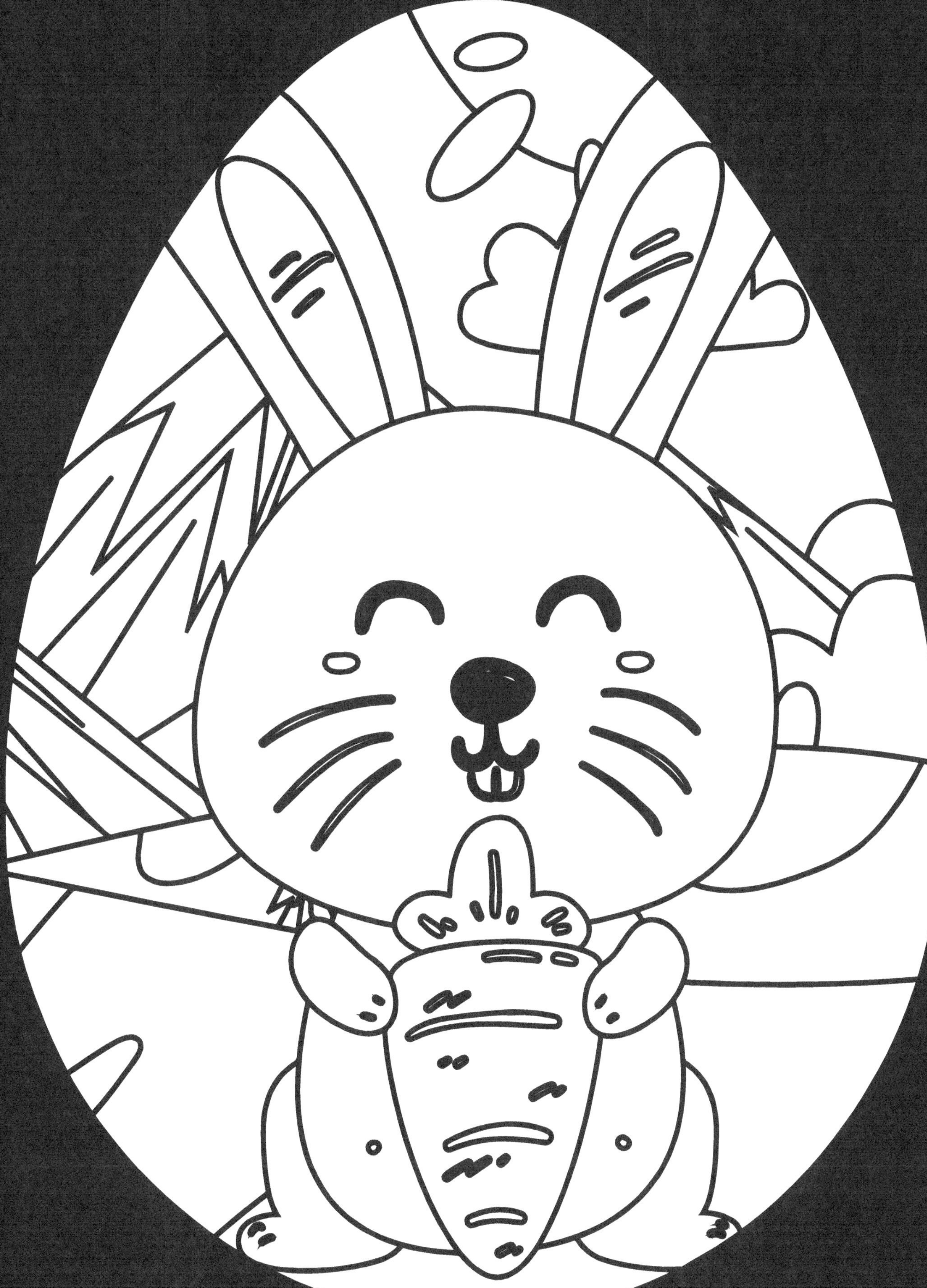

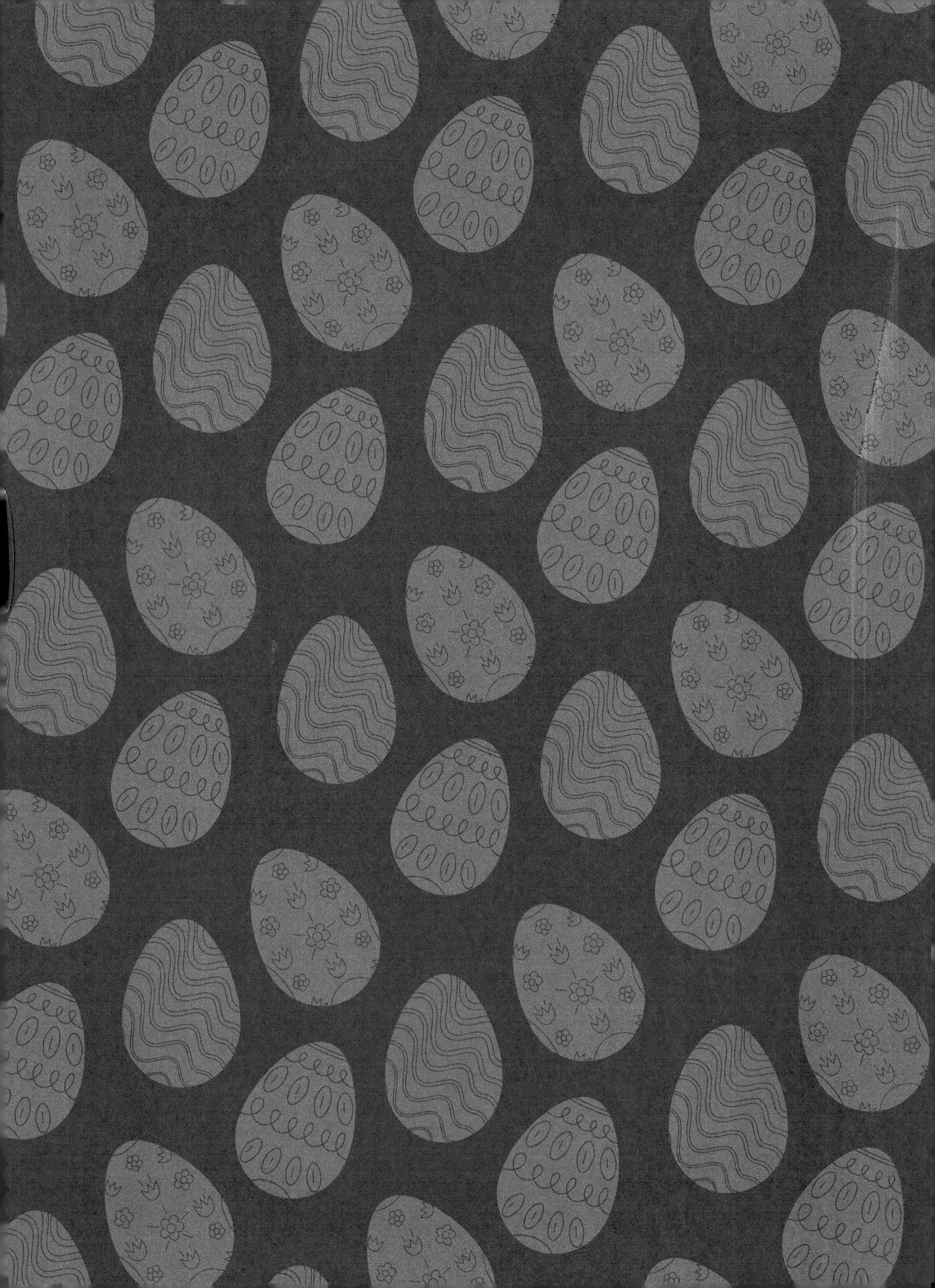